The Girlfriend Getaway Guide

Help Us Keep Making Girlfriend Getaways a Reality

Every effort has been made by the author and editors to make this guide as accurate and useful as possible. However, many things can change after a guide is published—establishments close, phone numbers change, facilities come under new management, etc.

We would love to hear from you concerning your experiences with this guide and how you feel it could be improved and kept up to date. While we may not be able to respond to all comments and suggestions, we'll take them to heart and we'll also make sure to share them with the author. Please send your comments and suggestions to the following address:

The Globe Pequot Press
Reader Response/Editorial Department
P.O. Box 480
Guilford, CT 06437

Or you may e-mail us at:
editorial@GlobePequot.com

Thanks for your input, and happy travels!

The Girlfriend Getaway Guide

*You Go Girl!
And I'll Go, Too*

Pam Grout

GUILFORD, CONNECTICUT

Copyright © 2003 by The Globe Pequot Press

All rights reserved. No part of this book may be reproduced or transmitted in any form by any means, electronic or mechanical, including photocopying and recording, or by any information storage and retrieval system, except as may be expressly permitted by the 1976 Copyright Act or by the publisher. Requests for permission should be made in writing to The Globe Pequot Press, P.O. Box 480, Guilford, Connecticut 06437.

Text design by Eileen Hine
Illustrations by Susan Miller

Library of Congress Cataloging-in-Publication Data
Grout, Pam
    Girlfriend getaway guide : you go girl! and I'll go too / Pam Grout.
       p.   cm.
    Contents: Home-front getaways — Spa getaways — Sports getaways — Road trips — Celebration getaways — Spiritual getaways — Shopping getaways — Luxury getaways.
    ISBN 0-7627-2697-0
    1. Female friendship—United States. 2. Women—United States—Psychology. 3. Women—Recreation—United States. 4. Vacations—United States. 5. Amusements—United States. 6. United States—Tours. I. Title: Girlfriend getaway guide : you go girl! and I'll go too. II. Title.

HQ1206.G793 2003
302.3'4'082—dc21
                                            2003054949

Manufactured in the United States of America
First Edition/First Printing

This book is dedicated to Mary Condron, Ivy Kahn, Nixie Ritter, Carol Keller, Suzanne Bonner, Bambi, Lee Ann Howard O'Brien, Susan Grapperhaus Faust, Karen Ingram, Joanne Owens, Crazy Marilyn, Wendy Druen, Michelle Shaw, Kristin Tilson, Barbara Luff (also known as red-headed Barb), Kitty Shea, Debbie Konomos (and all your sisters), Jenny Roesner, and every other girlfriend I have ever traveled with, lived with, or consented to participate with on any misguided adventure.

Contents

Introduction 1

Home-Front Getaways 21
How to "Get Away" without Leaving the Comfort of Your La-Z-Boy

Spa Getaways 41
Why It's Fun Getting Wrapped Up Like King Tut

Sports Getaways 61
How to Become a Surf Diva in Five Days or Less

Road Trips 79
Move Over, Thelma and Louise!

Celebration Getaways 93
How to Make a Wedding Shower Last Four Days

Spiritual Getaways 105
The Closest Thing to Heaven for Now

Shopping Getaways 121
Why God Created Credit Cards

Luxury Getaways 139
Life on the Trail of Julia Roberts

Your True-Life Tale 158
Journal Your Own Adventure

Index 163
About the Author 167

Introduction

> "THERE ARE MANY WAYS TO SPEND TIME WITH OUR FRIENDS, AND IF WE ARE COURAGEOUS, WE CALL UPON ONE ANOTHER TO MEET ON THE PLAYING FIELD AND DEVOTE OUR TIME TOGETHER TO THE HIGHEST END, WHICH IS NOT AN END, BUT THE FREEDOM OF EXPRESSION WITH WHICH EACH OF US IS GIFTED AT BIRTH."
>
> —Nina Wise, *A Big New Free Happy Unusual Life*

I have the best boyfriend in the entire known universe. He's tall, he's handsome, he adores my daughter. He even knows how to load a dishwasher. But no matter how perfect a boyfriend he is, he will never be a girlfriend. He will never—no matter how hard he tries—understand PMS or what it's like to be in labor or the exultation of finding the perfect black skirt.

The point I'm trying to make is: Girlfriends need girlfriends.

When we were in third grade, we knew this instinctively. We didn't care about boys—not really. It was fun to taunt them or to try to get them to kiss us at recess, but we knew that when the school day ended, it was our girlfriends we wanted to take home to eat Oreos and sit with us on our bunk beds. Our girlfriends were the ones who liked to talk, who wanted to be silly and giggle. All third-grade boys ever wanted to do was drive toy tractors around in the dirt.

Then puberty hit. Our priorities temporarily changed.

Until now . . .

This book is about the importance of girlfriends and about the things we can do to celebrate friendships with our closest pals. I'm talking about girlfriend getaways. Where it's just you and your girlfriends hanging out. Sometimes that's really simple—say, a tea party in the lobby of the local hotel. Other getaways are more complex—weeklong tramps through Mongolia, for example. The point isn't what you do or where you go. The point is simply this . . . we girlfriends need to get together.

Friends Forever

Girlfriends have been devising ways to get together for as long as we've been on this planet. We formed quilting bees. We canned vegetables together. We midwifed each other's children. We were part of the fabric of each other's day-to-day lives.

Today that's not necessarily the case. Between hectic work schedules, bulging Day-Timers, and Johnny's violin lessons, many girlfriends consider themselves lucky if they can find five minutes for a quick call on their cell phone.

Our busy lives have stripped us of the companionship, the support, the daily conversations we so desperately need (yes, need!). This is a big problem, girlfriends.

When we don't get together with the girlfriends we love most, the girlfriends who've propped us up over the years, the girlfriends who've reminded us to laugh, we become unbalanced and eventually unglued.

It doesn't happen right away. It's like the antique chair in the corner on which books, saxophone cases, coats, and fat Uncle Sylvester have been piled. At first it starts to wobble. And then it rocks. Eventually, if we don't pay some attention to that chair, it will fall in upon itself and the people and things it supports will come crashing down, too.

You can't pick up a women's magazine anymore without finding some kind of article about the importance of taking care of yourself. Well, I'm here to tell you that there's nothing that better takes care of yourself than a time-out with your girlfriends. If you ask me, there should be mandatory yearly events for every girlfriend over eighteen.

Karen, a professional speaker and author from Shawnee Mission, Kansas, credits a getaway she took with two of her friends for helping her cope with her first husband's untimely death from liver cancer. All convention told her to postpone the trip, to forget a drive across Iowa with two of her dearest friends.

But deep in her heart she knew that the support and the perspective she would get from the time with her friends would give her the strength to cope with the upcoming months.

"I was exhausted, depressed, and really needed time away. It was a sheer act of will to force myself to leave him and the kids to take just three short days for myself. But it was a blessing that I did. I came back refreshed, renewed, and ready to face anything," Karen says.

She met Mary and Jeanie in Des Moines. With video camera in hand, they took to Iowa's back roads with no particular destination in mind. As she notes, "We were merry wanderers." They did know that at some point they wanted to visit the baseball field that had been carved from a cornfield for the Kevin Costner movie *Field of Dreams*.

"We became sillier and sillier as the hours passed. By the time we got to Field of Dreams, we had decided that we would film a remake of the original movie," Karen says. "We enjoyed the sheer luxury of quiet time together and still had time for intimate late-night talks and laughing—lots of laughing. The best part was that it cost us next to nothing, just our time." Sure enough, her husband died a few short weeks later.

"Quite frankly," Karen says now, "I'm not sure I could have gotten through that difficult time without the wonderful, sustaining memory of that simple, silly trip across Iowa. It literally saved my life."

Today she keeps pictures from that getaway and others she's taken with her girlfriends next to her computer. Whenever she needs a reminder of what's important in life—whenever she needs to get centered, to put things in perspective—she looks at those pictures. They're big continual "ahh's". They keep her going. Better stress busters than yoga or breathing or even jogging.

A getaway with your girlfriends can restore your sanity. It can bring you back to your best self.

Calling All Girlfriends

"We all know the power, the glory and the thrill of connecting with other women. And it comes to us naturally. Hell, all we have to do is wait in line to pee in a public ladies' room. We'll tell each other about our bastard ex-boyfriend, our menstrual cramps and the factory outlet where we got this groovy outfit."

—Susan Jane Gilman, *Kiss My Tiara: How to Rule the World as a Smartmouth Goddess*

It's hard to pinpoint my first girlfriend getaway. Maybe it was the junior high ski trip with my sister and my cousin Peggy, where we laughed so hard about our ski outfits (Grandpa's insulated farm overalls) and our swan dives into the snow that each of us, at one time or another, peed our pants just thinking about it.

Or maybe it was the trip to Europe right after college when I bought a Eurail pass and convinced my friend Nixie, who was stationed in the army near Frankfurt, Germany, to travel with me to Greece. Even though that trip was taken twenty-three years ago, Nixie and I can still picture with perfect detail the nude beach we finally mustered up the courage to visit and the two motorcyclists without teeth who kindly took us from our seaside inn to the village to dance each night.

Back then these getaways weren't conscious decisions. There were no such things as Ya-Yas, no Sweet Potato Queens. We didn't know we were setting a precedent for something that today has an official name (a girlfriend getaway) and now, its own book.

All we knew is that very little in our lives was more important than these trips—and that the memories from these getaways are among the best moments of our lives. If a movie were ever made of my life, the highlights would undoubtedly come from one of the dozens of girlfriend getaways I've been on. There would probably be a scene in Breckenridge, Colorado, where six of my girlfriends, dressed in nothing but white hotel bath towels, show up on Crazy Biff's early-morning televised ski report. Another scene in which eight college friends are swing dancing on wall-to-wall roll-away beds in a hotel room designed to sleep two.

Very little in my life is poured in cement. But there are two annual get-togethers that won't change. Ask me what I'm doing the Friday before Easter and I'll tell you I'm committed to my date with Carol, Nixie and Bambi. Likewise, the KU–K State football game means a Saturday with eight of my college girlfriends. Nothing—not a date with Robert Redford, not a trip to the lottery office to pick up my million-dollar prize—could ever get in the way of these annual outings. That's how important they are to me.

The beauty of these getaways is that we never know exactly what's going to happen. Some years we're serious. We spend our time discussing miscarriages and wandering husbands. We console each other, remind each other that "everything is going to be okay" and that whatever crummy thing just happened "is not the end of the world." After all, we remember back when even worse things happened. And we got through those.

Other years we turn our brains off completely, spend our time together dancing and laughing. The year before last, for example, we ventured to Aggieville, a collection of college bars in Manhattan, Kansas, and danced with boys young enough to be our sons. We even convinced a couple of them to get down on their knees and sing "You've Lost That Loving Feeling." One year, we met an internationally famous crop artist and convinced him to pose with us in photographs.

The truth is we never know what to expect. Just that being with each other promises to be stimulating and life changing.

Besides these set-in-stone getaways, my girlfriends and I also plan out-of-town trips together. We've gone Oktoberfesting in Germany, golfing in the Ozarks, skiing in New Mexico. Right now we're negotiating a ski trip to Colorado with our kids—although I can guarantee that this will be different from former girlfriend ski trips where we, as one of us described it, met more men than moguls.

One year in Breckenridge (thanks to Carol, whom we quickly dubbed our fearless social director), we met a group of real estate bankers from Kentucky, a bartender named Moose with the Star of David shaved into his head, and an old college boyfriend of mine whom I didn't even recognize until he started doing the bump with Nixie. Some things you don't forget.

Girls-Night-Out Is Now Girls-Night-Out-of-Town

There are probably as many types of getaways as there are types of girlfriends. You can custom-design your own getaway at the resort (or bed-and-breakfast, hotel, or friend's house) of your choice. Or you can partake of special "girlfriend packages" that are zooming out of marketing directors' computers quicker than you can say Nia Vardalos. Resorts, hotels, and B&Bs are finally getting it—we girlfriends have money, and we're willing to spend it on traveling.

In fact, one of the hottest new vacation trends is getaways with the gals. The Four Seasons Hotel in Chicago (312–280–8400), for example, offers a "Girls Just Want to Have Fun" package. When you check in, you get a welcome basket with chick flicks, chick CDs, and spa products. Also included is a beauty makeover, discounts on Michigan Avenue, and free mimosas at Neiman Marcus. For the right price, concierge Abby Hart will also throw in tickets to *The Oprah Winfrey Show,* gourmet-cooking classes, front-row seats to the *The Vagina Monologues,* and Sunday brunch in the Seasons Restaurant.

The Lyons Victorian Mansion (800–78–GUEST), a bed-and-breakfast and spa in Fort Scott, Kansas, hosts old-fashioned slumber parties that include tea in the parlor, spa treatments, and Girls Night Out at the Barn where girlfriends, in their jammies, watch movies in big recliners with Orville's best popcorn.

In Seattle you can choose between the "Serenity and Sisterhood" package and the "Gals Just Want to Have Wine" package. The Alexis Hotel (206–624–8488) offers the serenity package that includes accommodations, a yoga mat for each girlfriend, private yoga instruction, spa treatments, and Queen of the Tub Kits that feature bath salts, scrubbers, and other goodies. Hotel Vintage Park (206–624–8000) offers the wine package, with overnight accommodations, a tour of Washington State's famous wineries, a picnic lunch on winery grounds, personal wine journals, an evening wine reception, and, of course, pedicure and manicures.

The Innkeepers of St. Augustine (Florida) Historic Inns (www.staugustineinns.com) reserve all twenty-five of their B&Bs for a women-only weekend each year. This three-night, four-day event includes scavenger hunts through art galleries, wine tastings, and many other exciting events. The first year, they sponsored an essay contest where women wrote in telling why they deserved such a getaway.

You get the point. There are plenty of girlfriend getaway packages out there. Many even give a percentage of proceeds to breast cancer research or some other women's cause. But rather than a book of listings (these packages change nearly as fast as Liz Taylor's husbands), this is a book of inspiration. I hope it convinces you that getting together with your girlfriends deserves top billing on your to-do list, and I hope it inspires you to pack your bags and say sayonara.

I've divided the book into eight chapters—eight types of getaways that you can plan with your girlfriends:

1. The first chapter is **Home-Front Getaways** (Or, How to "Get Away" Without Leaving the Comfort of Your La-Z-Boy). It covers weekend and weeklong getaways or what I call slumber parties for grown-ups. You don't have to get a passport to feel like you're getting away. Planning a weekend or even a single overnighter at a hotel can do wonders for your state of mind.

2. Second comes **Spa Getaways** (Or, Why It's Fun Getting Wrapped Up Like King Tut). While I'd probably be remiss in failing to mention the hourly Tai Chi, yoga, and hulaerobics classes most spas offer, the real reason we go to spas is so that attractive men can wrap our bodies in seaweed, herbs, and hot towels. And to collect

the lemongrass bath tablets and chamomile eye packs they leave on our pillows.

3. Chapter 3 is **Sports Getaways** (Or, How to Become a Surf Diva in Five Days or Less). Yes, I know, men are the ones who normally spend their vacations on a golf cart. But thanks to such girlfriends as Venus Williams and Mia Hamm, we gals can be potential Olympians as well. This chapter covers the dozens (maybe hundreds) of sports camps for women only.

4. Chapter 4 explains **Road Trips**, which are impromptu getaways taken in a car. Unlike Sunday drives or family vacations, road trips are done for no other purpose than to flaunt your nose at convention. Suitcases? Fagetaboutit! Itinerary? What's that? Destination? We'll know when we get there.

5. The next chapter covers **Celebration Getaways** (Or, How to Make a Wedding Shower Last Four Days). Whether you're toasting a new job, knitting booties for your sister's triplets, or getting ready to launch a marriage, a girlfriend getaway is two, three, or maybe a long weekend times better than a ho-hum tea party. You can still give gifts, but wow! Why not have the Eiffel Tower—or Bloomingdale's, for that matter—in the background of your photos?

6. Chapter 6 tackles **Spiritual Retreats** (Or, The Closest Thing to Heaven for Now). This is the serious chapter. The chapter that offers inspirational places to go when you just need to clear your head, when you've forgotten that life is about more than MasterCard bills and mortgage payments. Spiritual retreats, while often taken alone, can be even more meaningful when shared with a like-minded seeker—and admit it, that's more likely to be a girlfriend than your main squeeze.

7. The seventh chapter discusses **Shopping Getaways** (Or, Why God Invented Credit Cards). Every woman worth her pumps knows the last thing you need on a shopping excursion is a man. Men—even sensitive, quiche-imbibing men—do not understand the subtle nuances of *50 percent off, clearance sale,* and *buy one, get one free*. That's why we plan these trips with our girlfriends.

8. And finally comes **Luxury Getaways** (Or, Life on the Trail of Julia Roberts). This chapter will include such trips as the "Cartier Package" from Vancouver's Metropolitan Hotel, which includes a limo ride to Cartier, sterling-silver gifts, fluted champagne glasses, and chocolate-covered strawberries left in the room.

Each of these chapters gives a comprehensive rating of the four components of a successful G.G. (girlfriend getaway) that, as any "good girlfriend" knows, a G.G. has to have:

1. *A place to talk.* This is the most important component. We girls absolutely *must* have a suitable place to discuss everything from George Clooney's backside to the latest diet.

2. *A place to gawk.* So what if we're married? Good scenery (aka cute guys) is vital to every G.G.

3. *A place to rock.* It's not that we're going to be out partying every night (Hey, if component 1 is rated high enough, we may never leave the room), but it's essential that the "party" option be present should we choose to dance or to imbibe.

4. *A place to dock.* Just long enough to get pampered. We work hard the other fifty-one weeks of the year, so every good G.G. has to have a place to get massaged or wrapped in mud.

The main thing to remember is that most girlfriends don't really care what they do just so long as they have a chance to connect and to share.

In this book you'll also hear from lots of girlfriends, most of whom you haven't met. Yet. This book contains lots of what I'm calling "True-Life Tales" from girlfriends who have already discovered the joys of girlfriend getaways. I was surprised at how eager most girlfriends are to share their stories. When I put out the call for these tales, girlfriends from all over the country tracked me down to tell me what I already suspected: Girlfriend getaways have made a huge difference in their lives, sometimes the difference between sanity and insanity.

What follows is the first true-life tale, from Chris and her college friends, who may take the prize for doing this the longest and most consistently.

True-Life Tale

Sixteen Years and Counting

THE GIRLFRIENDS:
1. Chris, owner of new makeup company called Outstanding Faces.
2. Debbie, a friend from college.
3. Gerty, also a college friend.
4. Linda, ditto.

THE MISSION:
To preserve an incredible friendship that began in 1984 at the University of Lowell.

THE DESTINATIONS:
These girlfriends live in eastern Massachusetts, so most of their getaways have been in New England. They've been everywhere from luxury hotels to camping to a big stay-at-home sleepover when one of them had just had a baby.

THE GETAWAYS *(as told by Chris)*:
"My three closest friends and I have been going away annually for the past sixteen years. We usually go away one or two nights, at various times during the year.

"Our first weekend away was in the fall of 1985, to the village of Loon Mountain in Lincoln, New Hampshire. I don't think any of us envisioned that seventeen years later, we would have made going away an annual event, and that the four of us would remain each other's closest friends.

"We've been to many places, from camping in New Hampshire to the Ritz-Carlton in Boston, at various times of the year, scheduling around many life changes including marriage, pregnancies, jobs, and income (or lack thereof).

"Our most challenging travel experience was driving to New York City one December Friday in the early 1990s. About halfway there we got caught in the middle of a snowstorm, but made the decision to press on. By the time we reached the city, the snow had changed to rain, so we thought everything was fine. As we were sitting in the crowded hotel bar making our weekend plans, the nearby television was broadcasting news flashes about 'Manhattan under water' and the like.

"We quickly realized that most of the bar's crowd was stranded in the city due to the torrential rain. When some learned that we'd just arrived, by car no less, they looked at us like we were crazy! After seeing further broadcasts and getting more strange looks from others, we thought it might make sense to call home. Our spouses, boyfriends, and/or parents were grateful for our call: The news back home included horror stories about the city being flooded, shut down, streets closed, and people stranded. We just laughed at ourselves and proceeded to enjoy the rest of the soggy weekend.

"Over the years we've found that it really doesn't matter where we go; it's just that we make it happen. In fact, before we married our husbands, we've each explained that part of 'the deal' is the annual girls' weekend away. It's not that we do anything fancy: We simply enjoy each other's company, catch up on our lives, laugh, and just get goofy together! Our weekends typically include eating, relaxing, shopping, and sightseeing. Most years we've gone away for two nights, sometimes just one, and this year some of us extended the trip even longer.

"This year we celebrated Linda's fortieth birthday during our getaway on Martha's Vineyard. Linda is the first of the group to reach this milestone. As part of this occasion, Debbie brought along a tiara and flashy costume beads for Linda to wear, which she graciously did during dinner out one evening. We joked that we just started a new tradition: The tiara and beads shall be worn by each of us as we celebrate our fortieth birthday: Gerty's next!

"As part of Linda's present from the three of us, we assembled an album of pictures from past events and times we've shared together since college. We laughed at many memories and unforgettable quotes, how young we all looked in the 'early years,' and it was especially amusing to see all the iterations of our different hairstyles and lengths over the years.

"What's next? Not sure what's up for the coming year yet. However, we've just started discussing our twentieth annual getaway. While we don't yet know where we'll end up, we've decided to choose a location requiring a plane ride away. Except for New York, all our past getaways have been in New England, so we've been able to travel by car in previous years. While one can't count on many things in life, I expect these getaways and our special friendship will continue for many more years to come."

—*Thanks to Chris Vasiliadis for providing this True-Life Tale.*

Girlfriends You're Better Off Leaving at Home

1. Linda Tripp
2. Sandra Dee
3. Courtney Love
4. Marie "Everybody Loves Raymond" Barone
5. Imelda Marcos—where would you put all those shoes?

Anatomy of a Girlfriend Getaway and Other FAQs

"ANYTHING THAT LOOKS AS THOUGH IT WILL BE AS MUCH FUN IN MENOPAUSE AS IT WAS IN PUBERTY IS MY IDEA OF A SUCCESSFUL INSTITUTION."

—Stephanie Salter, *columnist*

During the writing of this book, I took a girlfriend getaway to Santa Fe, New Mexico, with two and a half of my friends. I say *two and a half* because Carol, one of our regulars, announced during the planning stages that she wanted to bring along her newly announced boyfriend, Fred, a not-quite-yet-divorced teamster.

Even though Fred was charming and looked like a cross between Sylvester Stallone and Tim Allen, we had to remind Carol that girlfriend getaways are called girlfriend getaways for a reason. Suzanne, Nixie, and I stayed at the Inn on the Alameda, an incredible hotel within walking distance of Santa Fe's famous plaza and just across from the entrance to Canyon Road. Carol and Fred stayed at a Holiday Inn across town.

Because this and other foibles can happen, I thought I'd use the trip as an example of how to plan a girlfriend getaway.

First, the seed gets planted. Somebody mentions that she's always wanted to see, say, the balloon race in Albuquerque, New Mexico. Or the Hearst Castle in San Simeon, California. Somebody else says, "You know, I'd like to do that, too."

And then somebody else finds out that Santa Fe, not too far from Albuquerque, also has a great Japanese health spa called 10,000 Waves, and that an exhibit of calla lily paintings will be showing at the Georgia O'Keeffe Museum. Before long we're convinced that being in Santa Fe is our ultimate destiny.

After countless e-mails and phone calls and much checking of schedules, a date is finally set. In our case we decide to meet in Santa Fe the weekend of October 10–12.

Be aware that once a date is set, somebody usually ends up dropping out. In our case Bambi, a shop teacher, has to decline because of a conference in Ohio.

The reservations are made. Even though Suzanne will be driving over from Flagstaff, meaning we'll have her car, we still want a hotel that's close to everything. The Inn on the Alameda (505–946–0544) is perfect. Not only is it in close proximity to everything Santa Fe is known for, but it also serves a to-die-for breakfast buffet, has several outdoor hot tubs, and hosts diet-breaking happy hours. In short, it's very comfortable and gives us plenty of excuses to sit around and talk—which really is why we're going to Santa Fe in the first place.

Nixie lives in Manhattan, Suzanne is from Arizona, and I live in Lawrence, Kansas. Even though we keep in touch via e-mail, nothing can replace the conversations that can be had in three nights and four days away from the kids and spouses. And in this case, while we visited several museums, walked up and down Canyon Road, bought beach wraps at the flea market, and sampled Santa Fe's well-known restaurants, mostly we chatted about mutual funds and when to tell our kids about sex, and about breast cancer and George W. and Carol's new boyfriend and Jamie Lee Curtis and what the *P* in the Myers-Briggs test means.

If you've never traveled with your girlfriends, keep in mind that you're going to be roommates for a while. Temporarily, at least, you'll be sharing a universe, teamed in making decisions on where to eat, where to park the car, where to find the best deals on Indian jewelry. It's often wise to sit down and talk turkey about your travel MOs before you take off. And remember, the fewer expectations, the better.

But, But

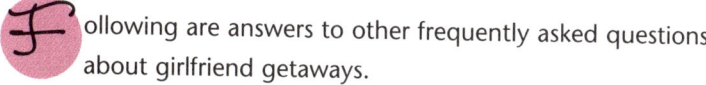

Following are answers to other frequently asked questions about girlfriend getaways.

1. **How do I explain it to my husband and family?** Granted, the first G.G. can be tough. Your significant others can't imagine why you'd want to go anywhere, especially on a vacation, without them. But once you've taken that first getaway, once they see how happy and refreshed you are upon your return, they'll be begging you to plan the next one. One man, on his wife's fiftieth birthday, even threw a surprise girlfriend getaway, inviting one friend from each of the five decades of her life.

2. **What if I can't afford it?** It takes very little money to get together with friends. But if you want to take a fancy trip, I suggest firing your shrink and using the money you save on therapy to pay for your trip. As far as I'm concerned, therapy and girlfriend getaways offer the exact same benefits. They both enlarge your life, they both bust up stress, and they both give you ample opportunities to talk about family and other life dysfunctions. Dare I add that the photos from girlfriend getaways are much more scenic than the view from a therapist's office?

3. **How often should I go?** Once a year is a bare minimum.

4. **What else do I need to know?** Sometimes it helps to have a name and props. For example, a group of six girlfriends from southern Missouri ski together every year. They call themselves "Chicks on Sticks." Another group of nine girlfriends from Chicago, who call themselves "Pearls Striving to Be Cultured," meet every month to try new things and to broaden their knowledge of culture. Of course, they wear pearls to all their meetings.

A friend of mine in North Carolina formed a Spinsters' Club one Valentine's Day when she and a couple of friends didn't have dates. They got together, ordered pizza, and shared "worst date ever" stories. These days, even though two of the three are married, the Spinsters get together at least once a year. Mostly, my friend says, "We just sit around and gab a lot. We talk about what each has been up to since last time, how 'far' we've come since way back then, and give each other advice (wanted or not). Usually there's a walk or shopping involved, and always there's eating. There's one particular bakery in Charlotte that has a great cake, and often one of those turns up.

"These two girlfriends are important to me because they share history. They knew me in my single days, in my not-so-great dating days, in my dated-a-nice-guy-but-it-still-didn't-work-out days, and in my falling-in-love-and-finally-marrying-the-right-guy days. They celebrate my successes.

"They were there for my wedding—where they helped out by becoming impromptu waitresses and serving the champagne for the toast—and they'll be there anytime I need to talk. The cool thing is we may not see each other for six months and only talk by phone infrequently, but when we do finally get together, we always pick up like we've never been apart. I don't have to see them a lot to know they are there and they care. Oddly, the three of us are so totally different that it's amazing we ever became friends at all, but that adds to the specialness of it."

Home-Front Getaways

How to "Get Away" without Leaving the Comfort of Your La-Z-Boy

> "NO MATTER BY WHICH CULTURE A WOMAN IS INFLUENCED, SHE UNDERSTANDS THE WORDS 'WILD' AND 'WOMAN' INTUITIVELY."
>
> —Clarissa Pinkola Estes, *Women Who Run with the Wolves*

Guys, for the most part, have one thing on their mind. Sports. When they plan a getaway, it usually revolves around golf, college football, or watching golf and college football on TV. This is all fine and good. For them.

But we girlfriends have better things to do with our getaways. At last count I came up with 3,987 things most girlfriends would rather do than watch a tiny white ball being knocked up and down perfectly mowed hills.

TALKING ★★★★

Talking—especially about your dreams and deepest aspirations—is the point of these getaways. Take Listerol. Your throat may get sore.

GAWKING ★★

Since weekend or weekly getaways by their very nature are short, gawking is not a crucial factor. But if you must, bring pin-ups of Matthew McConaughey.

ROCKING ★★★★

It's not your garden-variety dancing and beer-drinking rocking, but what could possibly be more stimulating than sharing the inner stirrings of your soul?

DOCKING ★

You probably haven't left your hometown so, unless you live with Martha Stewart, the docking is probably pretty marginal. But look at the advantages. It's dirt cheap. Your dresser won't be littered with travel brochures. And you don't have to spend significant time explaining to significant others who don't understand about Paris in the springtime.

For one thing, we girlfriends have important things to talk about. We have dreams that need airing, creative ideas that need expression. Girlfriends crave rituals, deep connections, and other meaningful experiences that—no offense—rarely take place on the 35-yard line. That's what this chapter is about: staging simple getaways that don't involve passports. These are getaways that can be done right in your very own living room. Or at least your hometown.

Sometimes that means going to the local Holiday Inn for an overnighter. A weekend with room service can do wonders for your state of mind. Take the right props (a Ouija Board, a good chick flick, or face paint) and you can fly all the way to the moon and back. Other home-front getaways include forming a group that meets weekly, or monthly, or every other Wednesday when you and your old college roommate write poems together at the local cafe.

Keep in mind that "getting away" is a state of mind. It simply means getting away from the normal routine. Girlfriend getaways, above all, lead you to a different way of thinking and being.

It's All in the Details

"YOUR LIVING ROOM IS A COVEN WAITING TO HAPPEN."

—Anna Johnson, *Three Black Skirts*

In *Divine Secrets of the Ya-Ya Sisterhood*, the Ya-Yas, four lifelong friends, survived divorce, alcoholism, even death by using humor and a sense of joy in the details of their lives. In the whole scheme of things, their lives were pretty ordinary. None of them was famous or had an earth-shattering career. None was a millionaire or even known outside their little burg of Thornton, Alabama. But boy, did those ladies know how to live. They turned those ordinary lives into something extraordinary. They didn't just fix dinner. They made a feast. They didn't just throw parties. They hosted galas. Everything they attempted was done with aplomb.

That's what a girlfriend getaway is all about. It's more than taking a trip or booking a plane reservation. It's about making a life. It's about throwing out ho-hum ruts and lifeless rituals.

Look up the phrase *joie de vivre* in the dictionary and you'll find a picture, to borrow an old Rodney Dangerfield joke, of my girlfriend Michelle. Every thing she does—and I've been watching her for a long time, since we shared lockers in high school—is done with a sense of sparkle. Every February, for example, she stages a Monty Python film festival. She makes costumes that RuPaul would sell his implants for, and throws parties where everyone comes naked except for raincoats.

She's a kindred spirit to Dame Edith Sitwell, who said, "I am not eccentric. I'm just more alive than most people. I am an electric eel in a pond of goldfish."

The vast majority of adults in this country are bored, lonely, and afraid. In fact, one of the world's biggest problems is that none of us knows how to have fun anymore. We're all wallowing in misery. One of the most radical things we girlfriends can do is have a good time, and to let other people know that having a good time is a good thing. As simple as that sounds, most people think "having fun" is a waste of time or, more accurately, something they have no control over.

But it's an intentional decision. We girlfriends get to make ourselves into who we want to be.

Weekend Getaways

You know that hotel you drive by every Tuesday on your way to the Indian deli? It has rooms to rent. And since you're a local and might even know the owner from the PTA, you can probably negotiate a great price for an overnight stay.

My daughter invited five girlfriends to a local hotel for her eighth birthday party. It wasn't even a mile from our home, but thanks to the pool, room service, and the absence of nagging moms (well, except one: me), Tasman and her friends might as well have been in Nigeria. We called it a "Come Jump on a Mattress Party" and sent out invitations on stuffed mattress ticking. The girls had a ball.

So keep in mind that hotels don't have to be situated next to an ocean to provide escape.

And while most hotels have interior designers, you might want to add your own decorating touches. Such as postcards or pictures from travel magazines. Or throw crepe-paper streamers over the TV.

You might want to pick a theme for your weekend getaway. Think of themes that appealed when you were in junior high. Maybe you'll want to

> ### Three Easy Meals for Your Family
> 1. The number for Pizza Hut.
> 2. A pyramid of Campbell's soup cans.
> 3. 1 (800) Hot–Hams will overnight a honey-glazed beaut straight from a Virginia smokehouse.

dance the watusi or apply temporary tattoos to each other's arms.

My very favorite theme is Show and Tell. As far as I'm concerned, all of us need Show and Tell on a regular basis. To stage a "Show and Tell Getaway," urge all your girlfriends to bring an item that means something special to them—something that represents their uniqueness. Ask them to read out loud the poems they've secretly written, or bring in some doodle they drew on the side of a Visa bill or the story they thought up while waiting at the dry cleaner.

Girlfriends still think things up. We just don't tell anyone. We don't think it's important. Not with diapers that need changing and toilet bowls that need scouring.

How much closer would we all be if we stopped long enough to honor each other in a circle of Show and Tell? If we listened to each other's stories, looked at each other's creations? We're all hungry for community. We need more ways to connect. Girlfriends still need Show and Tell. Literally.

We also still need story time, music time, nap time, and snack time. Probably even more than kids do.

My highest vision for girlfriend getaways is that communities of women would form "sacred circles." At these sacred circles girlfriends could not only discuss important aspirations and dreams, but also show each other their creations: their self-portraits, their poems, their balloon sculptures. Think of it as your own personal variety show.

Weekly Getaways

The potential for weekly get-together getaways is enormous. You can stage a mastermind group (in which you visualize handsome men and movie contracts with MGM for each other) or a "wild women" group (where you act outrageous for an hour or more every week). Or a writing group. Or a painting group. Or a let's-bitch-about-our-horrible-lives group. All you have to do is use a little imagination. I belong to a women's group called the Yo-Yos.

Unlike some women's groups where participants yammer on about the problems in their life, we Yo-Yos commit to doing something daring, bold, and outrageous each meeting. One week, for example, Lana, a fabric artist, brought some of her fancy dyes. We cleared Lynate's car out of her garage and tie-dyed our underwear. Now, whenever we get together, we wear our special underwear as a sort of secret password.

The Yo-Yos have also chalked poems on sidewalks, spray-painted grand statements on bridges (don't tell the Lawrence police), and hosted potlucks where each of us brought a new kind of sandwich we made up.

We meet every other Tuesday. Since all of us are moms, this is no small task. But it's worth every bit of effort.

So How Do You Find This Sacred Circle of Women?

Think of it like cheerleader tryouts. The girlfriends who win these coveted positions (and these are highly sought-after positions) are going to be "rah-rah-rahing" you every week or so. They're going to be believing in you, encouraging you, patting you on the back for faithfully showing up and being your bigger self.

Notice I didn't say *critic*, but *cheerleader*. This is an important distinction. The last thing you need right now is a girlfriend who's going to put her finger down her throat when she hears your poem about the neighbor's puppy, or one who tries to convince you that that black skirt needs a fuchsia belt to make you look thinner.

Uh-huh! *That* girlfriend needs to take a long vacation to Siberia. By herself.

If you feel a little funny about asking your girlfriends for this much time, remember that you are offering a gift. Not only will you be doing the

When You're Stuck on Discussing "Him"

A snoopy scientist once put a hidden microphone on women's conversations. He wanted to know what women talk about. The results were not pretty. He determined that 75 percent of women's conversations center on the opposite sex. This is not a good thing, girlfriends. Once we've gotten the "how you met" or the "who do you want to meet" out of the way, there are many, many topics infinitely better to spend our time on. For example:

1. What is your favorite constellation?
2. When was your first visit to the doctor?
3. What sport would you like to be good at?
4. What's your favorite city? If it's the one you're in, describe it. What do you like about it? Maybe it's the Polish bread maker down the street. Or the fact that all your cousins live there. Or because the magnolia trees are gorgeous in the spring? Have you really thought about this?
5. What's your favorite building in town?
6. Who is your favorite poet? You don't know. This is where the library card will come in handy. If you don't know, go find out. And remember, songwriters like the Indigo Girls and Bob Dylan are modern-day poets.

7. What's your favorite river? Tree? Flower? Don't forget to tell your girlfriends why you like these things—it will reveal great truths about yourself.
8. What are you good at? Don't forget things like building friendships or making banana bread. Maybe you're exceptionally good at keeping the peace. Or making others feel good about themselves.
9. What's your favorite color?
10. What was your favorite book as a kid?
11. Who was your favorite president?
12. What's your favorite letter? Number? Era? Planet?
13. In the movie *The Way We Were*, Robert Redford and his friend spent an enjoyable day naming their favorite day. Favorite year? Favorite age? Also, what was your favorite grade in school? Why?
14. What would you name a boat if you owned one?
15. Who was your favorite cartoon character when you were a child?
16. What is your nickname? What nickname would you like to have? Nickname of a coworker?
17. What's your favorite card game?
18. What movie would you like to see made?
19. What does an angel look like?
20. Who is your hero?
21. What do you think of questions like these? Why?

same thing for them (listening, seeing, and rah-rahing), but you are offering the gift of who you are as well.

These girlfriends get the privilege of *really* getting to know you. Not the you who got the shoplifting conviction in junior high or the you who flunked out of sixth grade. Those are petty things that you did as a human.

No, these girlfriends are getting a ringside seat to the you who's *really* you. The God you, the richer, deeper you whom you might not have had the privilege of getting to know yourself. And that, my friend, is a rare and priceless gift. Seeing the authentic, God-like side of a person always raises the one who witnesses to a higher level.

Often, we show up to our friends and family as our little selves, the selves who obsess, the ones who eat too much sugar. It's no wonder we have problems getting along. But the *BIG* you, the girlfriend you who's willing to stand naked and unafraid, gives nothing but gifts. Trust me! You will inspire your girlfriends. And they will be glad you asked. They will be grateful that they know you as they do.

Maybe you already know a girlfriend or two who is willing to join your sacred circle. If not, post a sign at the local theater or library or hobby shop. Run a personals ad. Someone is out there.

It's probably better to choose girlfriends you're not already in a rut with. No offense, but familiar relationships tempt us to stay in our ruts. These get-togethers are meant to be fresh, raw, and alive.

I could give you a lot of rules on how to do it, but I trust that this process of meeting and sharing with your girlfriends will happen naturally.

I *will* suggest that you make two commitments. Rule No. 1: You meet every week. Or month. Or whatever works for you. You're in charge of working out the details. At first this may seem like a pain—finding time to meet every week, carving out the space in your already bulging Day-Timer. But eventually there will be nothing more important. It's a little like the launching of a project. In the beginning you're not sure you *really* want to, but once you get going, it's a greased slide down Easy Street.

Rule No. 2: Never judge or critique each other's sharing. Yes, you share with each other—proudly, boldly—but never make comments or suggestions. You are here to encourage. Your job is to say "yay" and give brownie points for the fact that your girlfriends showed up and shared their hearts. Period. That's all that is important. Showing up. Sharing your heart.

Why do these sacred circles work? Some of us, unfortunately, have this slight little flaw regarding commitments to ourselves. Who are we anyway but the slimy slugs on the totem pole of life? But if we know that someone else (someone important to us) is counting on us to read a poem or perform a skit, we'll somehow find the time to do it.

I'll close with a true story I heard about a Sunday school teacher in Kentucky. One Sunday a new little girl named Tammy comes bounding into her classroom. Tammy is bright, vivacious, and happy, but she was born without a left arm. The teacher welcomes her, silently wishing she'd known Tammy was coming so she could have explained to the other children about the importance of being understanding toward those who are different. But before she can give it much thought, one of the boys is pulling hair, another is tearing leaves off a plant. To keep peace, she starts in on a familiar "finger play."

"Here is the church. Here are the people."

She stops suddenly, aghast that she could have been so insensitive. Then she looks over at Tammy—whose right hand, joined with the left hand of one of the girls in the class, is joyfully making a steeple.

Together, we can build most anything—a steeple, a play, a new way of being.

Half a Dozen or More Aliases to Give to the Front Desk

If you saw the movie *Notting Hill*, you know that people like Julia Roberts do not sign their real name when they check into a hotel. There is a good reason for this. You do not want your eleven-year-old son to call asking if you've seen his left soccer cleat. Or your boss wondering if you'd mind spending just an hour or so Saturday retyping his grocery list. For just this weekend, you are a nonperson. You have disappeared. That is why we give front-desk clerks aliases, aka fake names. For all intents and purposes for this weekend getaway, you are:

1. Wilma Flintstone.
2. Jean Ann Herkemsnort.
3. Betty Crocker.
4. Isadora Duncan.
5. Lilly of the Valley.
6. Britney Spears (if you choose this one, don't blame me if ten-year-old groupies line up outside your door).
7. Ginger Rogers.
8. Julia Roberts.
9. Thelma S.
10. Louise Johnson.

True-Life Tales

Revenge!

THE GIRLFRIENDS:
1. Lori, a never-married social worker who was more than a little shocked when her ex-boyfriend announced a wedding date to someone else.
2. Karen, a colleague-turned-friend whom Lori bonded with ten years ago at a national conference, where they spent much of their time riding the trolley around the city and talking about "life being a journey of the heart's desire."
3. Sherrie, a former employee of Lori's who regularly invites her to homemade dinners.
4. Tonya, a coworker for many years and recent neighbor. She and Lori share the goal of living ordinary lives in extraordinary ways.
5. Shawna, Karen's daughter.

THE MISSION:
To one-up that creepy former boyfriend of Lori's.

THE DESTINATION:
Walnut Valley Bluegrass Festival (620–221–3250 or www.wvfest.com) in Winfield, Kansas. For four days straight, five concert stages feature live acoustic music from 9:00 A.M. to midnight. Dixie Chicks, Laurie Lewis, John McCutcheon, Tom Chapin, and hundreds of other performers entertain the 20,000 folks who come from all over to camp near the Walnut River.

As good as the concerts are, lots of people never make it out of their campsites, which can sometimes be elaborate affairs complete with matching sofas and La-Z-Boys. Many come a good week earlier for Land Rush, to stake their sites along the river or under the same big sycamore they've been camping for years. Campsites have names—like the Blue Bayou, with its pond with an alligator or a turtle in it; or the Chicken Train Camp, host of chicken bingo, a clucking competition, and tie-dye Fridays where any camper can bring a T-shirt, a pair of underwear, or an old scarf and tie-dye it. Every year, it seems, the campsites get more elaborate and celebrated via dozens of camp competitions sponsored by the campers themselves. One of the campsites throws a salsa competition, another has a Friday parade, still another has a costume contest. Last year's winner was a Dorothy (from *The Wizard of Oz*) with tattoos from head to toe.

People stay up all night long and play music. There are guitars, banjos, hammer dulcimers, mandolins, and somebody always seems to bring a beat-up trumpet to play "Taps" or to start a rousing round of "Stella"—to which everyone responds by yelling "Stella!" right back. It's always a good time.

> ### THE GETAWAY:
>
> *"Admit it. Men aren't that much fun anyway. It's way more of a hoot to be hanging out your best girlfriend, doing facials, feasting on popcorn and good white wine and gossiping about the idiotic thing your date did at the office party last weekend. What a moron! Forget about him. Forget about all of them."*
>
> —Nancy K. Peske and Beverly West, *Cinematherapy*

Girlfriends are important 24/7, but there's one occasion when they become irreplaceable. You know what I'm talking about. Nothing comes in quite as handy as girlfriends when the man in your life decides that the twenty-two years you spent raising his children are over. When he determines that the cute young secretary with the short skirts is what the shotgun seat in his new red convertible needs.

When this happens, girlfriends are there to tell you some version of these truths:
1. The guy's a jerk.
2. You deserve better.
3. Somebody 100 percent more caring, handsome, and sexy is right around the corner.

And as long as they're embellishing these lies, you might as well be hearing them at a beach in Nantucket. Or at a hotel down the street, the one that you charge to your husband's credit card.

Your girlfriends might even help you come up with a ritual to purge and heal—which is exactly what happened to Lori, a social worker from Kansas City.

Lori was sure she had met the proverbial "one." Her beau, also a social worker, told her he loved her. He begged her to live with him, introduced her to his family, and promised to support her while she went back to grad school. They talked constantly of spending their "Winnebago Years" together.

Two weeks after she quit her job, the job he'd encouraged her to quit so he could support her through grad school, and two days before his birthday, the birthday she'd planned a big wingding for, he casually mentioned that he wanted to date a nurse he worked with. *You what?*

Injury was added to insult a few months later when his sister, a woman Lori had grown close to, informed her that Mike had given the nurse a ring. On September 21, it seems, he was doing the very thing he'd led Lori to believe he would be doing with her.

Needless to say, this was not good news. But did Lori let it get her down? No way. She did what any self-respecting girlfriend would do. She planned a weekend getaway with her closest pals.

Lori decided that since Winfield (as people call the Walnut Valley Bluegrass Festival) happened to fall on the same weekend as her ex-beloved's wedding, she would have her own wedding. So what if she didn't have a fiancé, or even a boyfriend? She would host what she called an unwedding. Yes, she had a dress (a $20 affair that she bought a thrift store), her friends had bridesmaid dresses (in a rainbow of colors, also purchased at thrift stores), and there was even a fountain, a guest book, a carpeted runway, and music (a band that was going to play "100 Ways to Make a Man Feel Pain," before Lori decided that this was about her and not about the man who'd left her behind). The whole campground was invited, and boy did they have one humdinger of a reception. Champagne was served. The main entree was Almond Joys, complemented by gummy worms, Nerds, and Dum Dums. Golf carts carried the bride around the campground.

• • • • • • • • • • • • • • • •

Blue, Blue, My World Is Blue

THE GIRLFRIENDS:
1. Nina, artist-author.
2. Sheilah, jazz vocalist.

THE MISSION:
To pull themselves out of the dumps.

THE DESTINATION:
To hell and back.

THE GETAWAY *(in Nina's words, from her book* A Big New Free Happy Unusual Life*):*
"My friend Sheilah called and told me she was to-h-h-tally depressed. 'Me, too,' I said, happy to have company. The one thing I cannot stomach when I am miserable is for a good friend to

call and tell me how fabulously happy she is because everything in her life is going so well. . . .

We landed on the notion of throwing a party—a depression party.

"We told our guests to wear black and we served black food; black caviar, black sesame crackers, black bean dip, black coffee, dark chocolate. We had black plates and black napkins and black candles. And when anyone asked how you were, you had to say you were terrible, horrible, awful, and complain about all the disgusting, demoralizing, deflating, disease-ridden events happening in your life.

"After only a few minutes of kvetching, people started to feel much better and when asked how they were, they were desperate to say, 'fine, I'm having a great time,' but we wouldn't let them.

"Finally, we could not utter one more word of bad news. And giddiness welled up inside us, and we put on loud music, and we danced."

• • • • • • • • • • • • • • • • •

Forty-Seven Years and Counting

THE GIRLFRIENDS:
1. Mary, mother of eight.
2. Seven wonderful and delightful friends of four decades, also stay-at-home moms, whom Mary met when she married a farmer from LeRoy, Wisconsin.

THE MISSION:
To offer support and friendship on a weekly basis.

THE DESTINATION:
A different friend's house each Thursday.

THE GETAWAY *(as told by Mary):*
"I originally met these ladies through one of our church organizations, way back in 1955. It met on a monthly basis and after the business meeting, a lunch was served and then we were free to socialize. Some just sat and visited, others opted to play cards, a game called Sheepshead. We had such a good time playing together that we decided to form a group to play each week. Since we were all young, stay-at-home moms, we played on Thursday nights, usually around eight.

"We alternated among each other's homes, and we never served a lunch, but offered a beverage. Through the years, some members of our group have left, others have joined, but there are five of us who are original. Three of them are sisters, and they always say I'm their adopted sister. You have no idea how good that makes an only child feel. Since all of us are now retired and our children are all grown, we now play in the afternoon, always on a Thursday.

"There aren't too many weeks in the year that we don't play. Win or lose, we always have a good time, just girl talk and never any gossip. Our menfolk had a hard time believing that. They just knew that there was a lot of laughter going on. From time to time we go out for lunch, usually to celebrate a birthday. These ladies have become very dear to me and I view them as my extended family. I know that I can count on them for support and prayers whenever needed. Playing cards is not the only thing we do as a group. Last night the three sisters gathered at my home and we sat around my kitchen table, chatted, had some dessert, and made Rosaries for the missions. Many of us are still active in our church, working together for fall festivals and still attending those monthly meetings that initially brought us together.

"The youngest member of our group is sixty-six, the oldest eighty-two. One of our ladies has never been married, and I am the only widow, but we all have something in common—that little deck of cards that brings us together each week and gives us so much pleasure.

"All of us look forward to Thursdays, no matter what the weather. Outside may be cold or wet, and the news on TV may be devastating, but there is love, friendship, and laughter at our weekly get-togethers."

THE VERDICT:

From Anne, Mary's daughter: "I can only speak of the group as a daughter, but I tell you the lessons I learned were priceless. I learned that Mom was entitled to a weekly time-out with her friends, and that that time was a priority and important; life went on without Mom for a couple of hours a week. I learned it was allowed and healthy to have friends of your own, and interests of your own, and opinions of your own.

"We also learned early on that if we wanted Mom to be at something, don't schedule it on Thursday night. She had a prior commitment, and she stuck to it. So did the rest of her friends—which in a small town, pretty much took care of our friends' moms, too. When the group met at our house, it was always around the kitchen table, and I know there was always laughter—over the cards and coins mostly. I learned that this weekly gathering of women was a very good thing for my mom and she looked forward to it. I know that when Dad died four years ago, all of them were there, and I know they provided a unique kind of support system that no others could."

—*Thanks to Mary Wondra for providing this True-Life Tale.*

Spa Getaways

Why It's Fun Getting Wrapped Up Like King Tut

"INDIVIDUALLY WE MIGHT HAVE BEEN ORDINARY WOMEN, BUT TOGETHER WE BECAME BETTE MIDLER THUMBING OUR NOSES AT PRUDENCE."

—Sue Monk Kidd, *author*

The real reason we plan girlfriend getaways is because we want to get together. Make that we *need* to get together. We need girlfriend getaways like pancakes need syrup, like big tops need belts. We need to scratch that itch we all have to talk without censoring, to blab without editing, to have somebody say, "You know, I feel the exact same way." When it comes right down to it, it doesn't matter—*really*—where we get away to.

TALKING: ★★★★

What better place could you find to chitchat than a big comforting hot tub or a private, fits-just-you-and-your-best-buddy steam room? Something about sitting there buck naked opens us up to really examining those issues that sometimes stay buried under to-do lists at home. Granted, it's rather tough to dis your boss while engaging in Down Dog—a yoga position—or to relate your great buy on army boots while counting reps on the Stair Master, but overall, spas rank sky high on the talk criterion.

 **ROCKING:** ★

Most spas roll up the bamboo mats after dinner. If dancing, adult beverages, and chatting up strangers rank high on your agenda, there are better getaways to strive for. The lone star ranking comes from the fact that heavy-duty party towns such as New Orleans and New York City also have spas. If you pick a spa in a strategic location, you can break out of the mud wrap after dinner, party hearty all night, and be back in the lobby just in time for that first aerobic nature walk.

 **GAWKING:** ★

Well, needless to say, most of the gawking potential involves naked women wrapped in bath towels. Not only can this be disturbing to the old self-esteem, but it's not the type of scenery we gawking girlfriends had in mind. The good news (and the reason spas do deserve one measly star in the gawking category) is, men are starting to spa in record numbers. According to a study by the International Spa Association, 24 percent of spa customers are of the male persuasion. And we must not forget that there are some pretty saucy male massage therapists, some who have been known to revitalize the sexual imagination as well as the left shoulder blade. But overall, there are much better scenic getaways.

 DOCKING: ★★★★

Let's just say that at most spas, the amenities are to die for. And since you are getting away for no other reason than to pamper both your body and your soul, it's time for all girlfriends to repeat after me. Ready?

I deserve to be pampered.
I deserve candles by my bathtub.
I deserve lemongrass soap next to my sink.
I deserve freshly baked cookies on every counter, truffles on my pillow, and a concierge who remembers my name.

But I figure as long as we're going, we might as well go somewhere cool. That's what this chapter is about. Getting away to one of the coolest places in the known universe—a spa. That's spa as in *soak-away-your-cares,* as in *peel-away-those-wrinkles,* as in *wipe-away-that-old-fashioned-stressed-out-way-of-being.*

In fact, a getaway to a spa has the potential to completely repair your life. The communion with your girlfriends heals the inner you. The manicures, facials, and skin peels heal the outer. Come back from a spa getaway and you're practically a perfect human being.

The Spa Who Loved Me

Twenty years ago the only people who went to spas were folks like Marilyn Monroe and Joan Crawford, famous and rich people who needed to drop pounds or rejuvenate their complexions before their moviegoing public spotted them in, well, *public.* But now, thanks to the fact that practically every resort known to woman has added at least a massage therapist, spas are pretty easy things to get away to. Even Schoenchen, Kansas (pop. 201), has a spa. Granted, it was originally a nineteenth-century limestone barn, but like most spas it has European facials, more than one type of massage, and something called stone therapy.

And of course if you're not already familiar with day spas, those ubiquitous businesses that used to be called beauty shops, all I can say is, "Where have you been the last few years?" Any beauty shop worth its perm solution has added at very least a manicurist and a clinical aesthetician.

The number of spas in the United States has doubled in the last three years, and in 2001, for the first time, spa revenues surpassed those of theme parks and movie theaters. You can pick just about any location—your home city, one of the coasts, even a foreign country—and I guarantee there will be a spa to get away to.

Perhaps the better question is, "How much do you want to spend?" If money is no object (maybe you're one of those celebrities I mentioned earlier), there are plenty of lavish, top-notch destination spas that will pamper you, feed you low-fat gourmet meals, and give you lessons on eliminating stress—although (and I speak from personal experience here) if I could afford $5,000 for a week of spa treatments, what possible areas would be left to stress over?

If you're like me and money *is* an object (in fact, an object you spend a great deal of time concentrating on), you might want to look for bargain spas. The lobby might not be as fancy and there may only be five kinds of massages instead of eighty-two, but overall there are some good spas out there that won't preclude sending your oldest to college someday. Many spas offer discounts if you bring a girlfriend. Ask for even bigger breaks if you bring three or four.

If you're totally broke and can't even afford an hour at a day spa, I've also included a section for creating the spa scene at home. But for now, let's assume you're going to a spa outside your bathroom. What exactly are you looking for? If it's a full-fledged getaway (as in *real time away from the kids*), you probably want a destination spa or a resort spa. If you just want to catch up with a couple of busy friends, pick a day spa that's right in your neighborhood or a club spa where you can soak together after an aerobics class.

While I'd love to put every possible spa right here in this little book, I would be ninety-eight by the time I finished compiling the list, and the book would be so heavy you'd need more than a massage therapist (perhaps a doctor?) to repair the damage to your back. There are more than 9,000 spas in the United States alone.

According to the International Spa Association (ISPA), spas can be broken down into seven distinct categories:

1. Club spas. These spas are disguised as fitness facilities—you know, those places where you work out or play golf or racquetball. They're great if you just want to spend the afternoon gossiping with coworkers. But if you're looking for a long-term getaway, club spas have a definite downside: They don't offer rooms. You'll have to book those separately.

One example of a club spa is the Sedona Racquet Club (100 Racquet Road, Sedona, Arizona, or 928–282–4197). Needless to say it has tennis courts—eight of them that come with all kinds of clinics and tournaments—and it has a fitness center with yoga and Pilates classes. But keep on stretching that neck in yoga and you'll also notice the on-site Oasis Health Spa. It has three massage rooms, a facial room, and a full-service hair salon. You and the girls can have your bodies wrapped in that beautiful red Sedona mud, have a mini Thai honey facial, or enjoy a healing oxygen treatment. There's even a VacuStep that, at last report, was said to burn fat and eliminate cellulite.

2. Cruise ship spas. For years cruises were the last place you'd go if you wanted to get in shape. Usually you spent more time in lavish buffet lines than in the vessel's tiny gyms, which if you were lucky might have a Stair Master. Not so anymore. Today's cruise lines have installed everything from steam rooms and saunas to flotation tanks. Treatments range from traditional Swedish massage to crushed-pearl facials. On Seabourn Cruises, for instance, masseuses even walk around giving free neck, shoulder, and foot massages to sunbathing passengers.

Perhaps the best cruise spa is Cunard's new *Queen Mary 2* (800–728–6273 or www.cunard.com), making its debut in December 2003. They've teamed up with Canyon Ranch, a leading purveyor of spa resources, to provide almost everything its flagship resort in Tucson has for the ship's 20,000-square-foot SpaClub—twenty-four massage, body, and skin-care treatment rooms; a gym and weight room; a juice bar; a therapy pool; a whirlpool; and of course a Thermal Suite complete with an herbal sauna, a Finnish sauna, a reflexology basin, and an aromatic steam room.

And naturally there will be air-bed recliner lounges, neck fountains, deluge waterfalls, air tubs, and body massage jet benches. Also on board will be the exotic Rasul Ceremony, a Canyon Ranch SpaClub signature treatment. This medicinal mud and steam treatment, which takes place in an ornately tiled steam chamber, is derived from an ancient cleansing ritual. Canyon Ranch will also offer onboard presentations and workshops on stress management, smoking cessation, healthy aging, and disease prevention.

3. Day spas. As I mentioned, day spas are everywhere. To find one in your neighborhood, check out SpaFinders Web site (www.spafinder.com). Plug in your zip code and you'll get detailed descriptions of your many local day spas.

4. Destination spas. You go there, you eat there, you work out there. You come back beautiful.

The Golden Door (800–424–0777 or www.goldendoor.com) is the quintessential destination spa. Set on 377 beautifully manicured acres 40 miles from San Diego, it is the spa to which all others bow. Opened in
1958, back when most people had never even heard the word *spa*, it caters to the serious spa-goer. It also caters to people who don't have finances as one of their stressors. Its signature, seven-day getaway starts each Sunday

Spa Speak

*L*ike everything else, spas have their own lingo. For the sake of your well-being (yes, that's one of the spa terms), it's wise to get it down. Otherwise you'll be eating seaweed (spa cuisine) when you really wanted a double cheeseburger. Here are more important terms to master:

1. **CLINICAL AESTHETICIAN.** She's the gal who pops your blackheads. But even if you can't pronounce *aesthetician,* don't dare call her a blackhead-popper. Her degree, the one that's undoubtedly framed and hanging behind her chair, probably says something like "certified skin care specialist."

2. **DETOXIFICATION.** *Detox* for short, this process gets rid of everything that no longer serves you. Fasting, lymph massage, steam baths, and overnight in the klinker are just a few methods for detoxification.

3. **"GOOD GOLLY, I'M A HOT TAMALE."** This is an ***affirmation***— something you say loudly and proudly every time you look in the mirror. You might have heard it called positive thinking. Call it what you want, but affirmation works. It's why athletes and Andrew Carnegie types use affirmations to prepare for big gigs. What you think about and what you talk about is what you become. A good spa works not only on your physical demeanor, but also on the one thing that really counts—your inner demeanor.

4. **HOLISTIC.** It's hard to find a spa these days that doesn't throw out this term at least three or four times per minute. In a nutshell, it means that all parts of you are in balance. Your physical, mental, and spiritual health work together like a finely oiled top.

5. **MEDITATION.** Anything that relaxes your body and tells that annoying "monkey mind" to shut the heck up. (And what's the "monkey mind," you ask? For the answer, see the sidebar on page 115.) Scientists tell us

that meditation decreases your heart rate and blood pressure and increases your creativity and psychological well-being.

6. **PILATES.** Courtney Cox, Minnie Driver, and Julia Roberts are just a few of the stellar somebodies who use this seventy-year-old exercise treatment that focuses on flowing movement, concentration, and breath.

7. **SPA CUISINE.** Fresh, natural food that's low in fat and cholesterol. It's pretty much everything McDonald's isn't.

8. **TAI CHI.** An ancient Chinese art that incorporates slow, deep breathing with movements that relax your muscles and strengthen your body.

9. **THALASSOTHERAPY.** This treatment uses seawater (and all its vitamins and minerals) to heal you up.

10. **YOGA.** You may have noticed the radical transformation in Madonna over the last few years. Motherhood is certainly part of it, but yoga—an ancient practice that uses movement and breath to control, stretch, and tone the body—has also played an important role in toning down the Material Girl.

---

when Golden Door limos pick customers up at the airport. Meals, classes, treatments, and your own personal exercise therapist are all included. They even throw in a yukata (a Japanese cotton robe), warm-up clothes, and your own private guest room complete with shoji screens, CD players, outdoor decks, and private gardens.

Nonprivate gardens, the ones from which many of your meals are plucked, crisscross the secluded California countryside, along with organic orchards, waterfalls, and mountain trails. There are also meditative sand gardens, fountains, and a rare collection of antique stone lanterns. The Golden Door is modeled after the ancient honjin inns of Japan, restorative resting places for travelers after long and strenuous journeys.

If you have too many girlfriends, this one won't do, namely because it can only accommodate thirty-nine customers a week. On the positive side, each of the girlfriends you *do* bring will get four staff members taking care of her. No wonder the *Robb Report, Zagat Report,* and readers of both *Condé Nast Traveler* and *Travel & Leisure* have chosen the Golden Door as el numero uno spa in the country.

5. *Medispas.* Is the doctor in? At a medispa the answer is often yes. Spa therapies are combined with medical therapies to give you an overall boost. Get lucky enough and your insurance company might even chip in. Unlike some spas that offer three gourmet "squares" a day and only fifteen minutes of semi-aerobic exercise (the only thing that gets a workout is your liver), medispas are guaranteed to return you to real life as a healthier, more committed individual.

The Heartland Spa (800–545–4853 or www.heartlandspa.com), a converted dairy farm that lies 80 miles south of Chicago, is the perfect example of a medispa. It specializes in lifestyle makeovers and, yes, medical personnel get involved. Dietitians, nutritionists, and even doctors from Iroquois Memorial Hospital work with the spa team to give you an inner diet assessment and a personal nutrition counseling session. You get pampered, of course (I wouldn't dream of including a getaway where you didn't), but you also learn things that could conceivably make your life a whole lot better. The word of the day is *wellness*. They offer special rates if you bring a companion—and remember, it's easier changing your lifestyle when a friend gets involved.

6. *Mineral spring spas.* These are my favorite because they're less contrived. They're built around natural mineral or thermal springs. Many, although now updated, have been around since Christopher Columbus.

A good example is Rio Caliente (800–200–2927 or www.riocaliente.com), a destination that also happens to be one of those bargain spas I mentioned earlier, located just 25 miles from Guadalajara, Mexico. A week at this casual, comfortable, leave-your-makeup-at-home spa is six times cheaper than the Golden Door.

It's also built around a primeval volcanic hot springs. It has everything a girlfriend could ask for—reasonable prices (they even give discounts for bringing friends), beautiful scenery (it's surrounded by the Sierra La Primavera, a magnificent belt of volcanic mountains), comfortable accommodations (each of fifty cottages features handmade ceramic tiles, handcrafted furniture, and fireplaces), and exciting classes. Depending on the month, you can have your tarot cards read, get your astrology chart plotted, or enter a guitar contest. At any time you can dip in the four pools or natural steam room. There's always massage, beauty treatments, and excellent food. There also happen to be a hundred kinds of birds and a tequila factory close by.

7. *Resort hotel spas.* The resort, like the cheese, stands alone. A spa is just an added benefit—like, say, a golf course or an on-site Bloomingdale's. These are perfect if not all your girlfriends want to spend every waking moment getting their bodies and psyches pummeled.

A good example is the Allegria Spa at Park Hyatt Beaver Creek Resort (970–748–7500 or www.allegriaspa.com). In case its title didn't give it away, let me say right up front that this is a resort spa. A really great resort spa. Not that the spa couldn't stand on its own. It has 20,000 square feet, all inspired by Feng Shui principles, twenty-one pastel treatment rooms, indoor and outdoor Jacuzzis, sauna and steam rooms, and all the latest equipment.

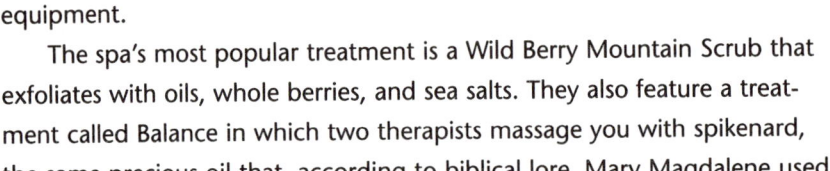

The spa's most popular treatment is a Wild Berry Mountain Scrub that exfoliates with oils, whole berries, and sea salts. They also feature a treatment called Balance in which two therapists massage you with spikenard, the same precious oil that, according to biblical lore, Mary Magdalene used to anoint Jesus' feet. It's the best place I know for enhancing your chi.

And keep in mind that there's a reason Greta Garbo dunked her head in icy water every morning. Cold constricts blood flow and tightens the skin. So what better place to spa than in the mountains where, in the winter, you'll naturally look more beautiful?

The resort that goes along with it is as good as it gets. This upscale ski resort (even ritzier than Vail) has every amenity you could ask for. Think *rustic;* think *elk heads and animal prints.*

Where Do I Begin?

There are lots of ways to find a spa. You can always call Spa Finder. Not only do they have an 800 number (800–255–7727) with friendly operators who will fill you in on what's available, but they're usually pretty hip on which discount packages are applicable the week you want to go. They also have a great Web site (www.spafinder.com).

Destination Spa Group (www.destinationspagroup.com) offers ready-made spa vacations, including discounts, at a select number of spas primarily in the United States. You can read spa overviews, learn about special offers, and book online on this site.

About.com (www.spas.about.com) offers one of the most comprehensive spa sites on the Web. Like the rest, it can help you find the right spa, but this site also teaches spa terminology. Be sure to check out the special values and freebies sections.

And yes, many spas offer special G.G. packages such as the "Girlfriend Getaway Package" at Spa Ojai at Ojai Valley Inn (800–422–6524 or www.ojairesort.com). Included in the deal are hotel accommodations for four girlfriends, two fifty-minute spa treatments per person, and your choice of one group activity such as art classes, golf clinics, wildlife cruises, horseback riding, or guided kayaking.

Saddlebrook Resort and Spa (800–729–8383 or www.saddlebrookresort.com) in Wesley Chapel, Florida, offers "Mom and Me" packages with two nights' lodging, daily lunch and dinner, a welcome package of chocolate and spa goodies, four spa treatments each, and a souvenir photo to take home.

The World's Wackiest Spa Treatments

F ar be it from me to knock anything that makes me look younger. But c'mon, some of these spa treatments are . . . how can I be polite here? . . . downright ridiculous. Thanks to what's known in the spa business as "signature treatments," things have gotten a little out of hand. Using local lore and local products, they add wildflowers, cactus, sage, and green tea to various massage therapies. It's one thing for an oceanside spa to offer thalassotherapy (using naturally salted seawater), but when spas, in their efforts to have a one-of-a-kind signature, start using cherries, sugarcane, barbecue sauce, and even chocolate, you have to wonder if they're not taking things a little too far.

But the treatment that takes the prize for wackiest of all may be the skin cream that's made from Japanese nightingale droppings. Yes, they actually use bird dookie and have the chutzpah to claim that it lightens and smooths the skin. Japanese geishas, they claim, have been using it for centuries. Besides the fact that I have no desire to look like a Japanese geisha, I also don't relish the idea of applying bird doo-doo to my face, even if it *is* dried, beaten to a pulp, sanitized with ultraviolet light, and mixed with essential oils.

Home Sweet Spa

Considering that a week at the Golden Door costs more than my car, it's prudent to also consider a spa getaway at home. First, send all children and significant male others elsewhere for the weekend. Then invite all your friends over and haul out the nail polish, the mud masks, the hair spray. Do each other's nails, slurp fruit smoothies, and give each other makeovers. Maybe you'll even want to go all-out with blue eye shadow, red lipstick, stick-on jewels, and fake eyelashes.

While your bathtub (pretend whirlpool) probably won't fit more than one girlfriend at a time, there are lots of beauty treatments you can make together (see the recipes below). And don't forget to massage each other's shoulders.

Veggie-Me-Mask

This recipe uses the beta-carotene and antioxidant vitamins from carrots, along with the calcium and protein in heavy cream, and vitamin E from avocado to improve texture, diminish age spots, and rebuild collagen.

YOU'LL NEED:

1/2 cup heavy cream
1 carrot (cooked and mashed)
1 avocado (peeled and mashed)
3 tablespoons pure honey

HERE'S WHAT YOU DO: Combine the ingredients in a bowl and spread over your face and neck. Relax for fifteen minutes. Rinse with cool water.

Source: www.ArizonaSpaGirls.com by Lara Piu and Lisa Kasanicky. The Spa Girls have a wonderful Web site that explains anything and everything having to do with spas—especially spas in Arizona. Sunny and Jasmine, the quintessential spa girls, certainly know how to put on a good spa party. My thanks to them for providing this and the following recipes.

Tried-and-True Cucumber Soak

Okay, it's not just an old wives' tale . . . cucumbers really do help relieve puffiness, sore eyes, and eye fatigue. Cukes have a high water, silicon, and salt content, which helps soothe and cool eyes. The salt helps draw excess water from the tissue surrounding the eyes, reducing puffiness. They also help to tone and firm the skin around the eyes.

YOU'LL NEED:

Sliced cucumbers
Bowl of ice

HERE'S WHAT YOU DO: Allow the cucumber slices to cool on the ice for a few minutes. Place a cucumber slice over each eyelid and relax for ten to fifteen minutes.

Source: www.ArizonaSpaGirls.com by Lara Piu and Lisa Kasanicky

Heavenly Bodies Lotion

Your body will feel just like it's fresh out of heaven after you treat yourself to this recipe!

YOU'LL NEED:

1 small container of coconut oil
15 drops of your favorite essential oil

HERE'S WHAT YOU DO: Microwave the coconut oil, uncovered, for thirty seconds. (On the stovetop, place the tub inside a large pan with water and heat on low until liquefied.) Add the essential oil. Stir, re-cap, and place in the refrigerator for fifteen minutes. Generously apply all over your body (but not your face) and cover up with old sweats and socks (the oil may stain).

Source: www.ArizonaSpaGirls.com by Lara Piu and Lisa Kasanicky

Jasmine's Tired Tootsies Remedy

Daily grind wreaking havoc on your feet? This recipe is just what the SpaGirls ordered. Before you go to bed tonight, rub it in and give those tired tootsies what they want and need.

YOU'LL NEED:

- 1/2 cup unscented body cream
- 12 drops essential oil of peppermint
- 5 drops essential oil of lavender

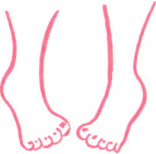

HERE'S WHAT YOU DO: Add the peppermint and lavender oils to the body cream. Stir and store in a plastic or glass container. To use, first massage your feet with a roller, soak in warm soapy water, then remove heavy calluses with an exfoliant. When you're done, rub on the foot cream, lie down on a bed, and elevate your feet with a few pillows.

Source: www.ArizonaSpaGirls.com by Lara Piu and Lisa Kasanicky

True-Life Tales

Sisters Reunite

THE GIRLFRIENDS:
1. Yours truly, back in her Bohemian gypsy phase.
2. My sister, Becki, a systems analyst for Gulfstream Aerospace.

THE MISSION:
Becki's husband, Dave, had a free airline ticket that had to be used by a certain date. He couldn't get away and Becki, who has five weeks of vacation, decided to take advantage of her sister's (that's me) new residence—which judging from past residences, wasn't likely to last very long. Come on out to California, I said. Let's drink some wine and check out Sonoma Valley. Free airline ticket. Free room. What idiot would say no!

THE DESTINATION:
Sonoma Mission Inn and Spa (707–938–9000 or www.sonomamissioninn.com). Built in 1927, this venerable old spa has real underground hot springs. It's designed to look like the old California missions, with arcades and bell towers. And it's located in the heart of Sonoma Valley, where there are wineries to tour, Calistoga mud baths to take, and Jack London's old home to visit.

THE GETAWAY:
Becki and I, who live on opposite ends of the country, spent most of our time catching up. Despite the fact that there were nonstop classes and tourist attractions, we opted to spend most of our time

talking. From sunup to sundown, we discussed such important issues as:

1. How is Dad's heart?
2. What have you heard from Sue Ann and Kennalea?
3. What are Micah and Zach [her kids] up to these days?
4. How is your marriage?
5. How is my love life?
6. What do we want to be when we finally grow up?

You know, the usual conversations. We took yoga classes, soaked in the hot springs, and ate healthy California cuisine. It was relaxing, fun, and a perfect way to use up a free airline ticket.

•••••••••••••••••

Gawking Anomaly

THE GIRLFRIENDS:
1. Yours truly, in my monthly travel column days.
2. Jen, daughter of an old boyfriend.

THE MISSION:
To relax and to see how the "other half" lives.

THE DESTINATION:
La Costa Resort and Spa (800–854–5000 or www.lacosta.com), an upscale spa near San Diego.

THE GETAWAY:
I want to make one thing perfectly clear: Jen and I barely peeked at Sylvester Stallone. We were busy sunbathing at the pool, after all. We couldn't have cared less that the famous superstar was golfing the north course at La Costa Resort and Spa only 50 yards away. We didn't really stare. In fact, we hardly noticed his blue golf shirt,

his tanned physique or the fact he looked a whole lot better than he ever looked in *Rocky.* Honest.

No, the real reason Jen and I were at La Costa Resort and Spa was to escape our regular routine back home. We were there to plunge into milk baths, relax with herbal wraps, and alternate among whirlpools, one for every temperature.

And since every shower stall featured a different flavor, we came back from our adventure cleaner than we ever have been or ever will be again. But how could we resist? The peach stall had peach shampoo, peach conditioner, peach lotion . . . with similarly coordinated items in the coconut stall, the lemon stall, and the special spa fragrance stall. Need I say more?

When Barbara Walters's ex first bought the 400 acres outside San Diego, he envisioned golf courses. While he certainly got a couple, (did I mention Stallone was golfing on the north one the Saturday we were there?), he also got a partner who'd recently visited Baden Baden, a spa in Germany. Before long La Costa became the spa for movie stars to have their bodies massaged, moisturized, tanned, loofahed, and wrapped in herbs.

La Costa offers lots of other options, as well. With its two PGA golf courses (oh, did I tell you Sylvester Stallone was golfing on the north course the Saturday Jen and I were there?), twenty-one tennis courts, bike trails, and daily exercise classes starting at 8:00 A.M. with a power walk and continuing until 4:00 P.M. with yoga, you can get some exercise in between all that gossip.

● ● ● ● ● ● ● ● ● ● ● ● ● ● ● ●

To Spa or Not to Spa: That Should Not Be the Question

THE GIRLFRIENDS:
1. Diane, a grieving wife whose husband had just been diagnosed with stage-four cancer.
2. Two of her best buddies.

THE MISSION:
To get Diane's mind off problems back home.

THE DESTINATION:
Sol Day Spa at Steamboat Springs Resort in Colorado (970–871–9785 or www.solspa.com).

THE GETAWAY *(as told by Diane):*
"My husband was diagnosed with stage-four cancer in March of this year. Everything we had wished for suddenly changed! I already had a trip planned to Sol Day Spa in Steamboat Springs, Colorado, with two of my friends, and after much agonizing decided to go ahead. I had been there once before and was scheduled for their "NIRVANA" package. I couldn't wait for an entire day of relaxation. I used to think that going to a spa was just pampering. Now I know that it is necessary for relaxation and positive mental health! Everyone at Sol Day Spa was great. I cannot decide which treatment is my favorite—either the Anti-Aging Facial or the Mountain Rain Vichy Glow. What I know for sure is that I was so relieved and so much calmer after our day together. We ordered champagne with lunch and sat in their Client Resting Room and stared into the fireplace. Real life seemed so far away. We just enjoyed being together and laughing. Laughing felt good. I will definitely be back as soon as I can! It has been a long seven months, but the chemotherapy seems to have worked—and my husband is doing fine for now.

Sports Getaways

How to Become a Surf Diva in Five Days or Less

> "GIRLFRIENDS JUST GET IT. THEY UNDERSTAND HOW YOU FEEL AND WHAT YOU'RE GOING THROUGH. THEY HELP YOU SEE THE BIG PICTURE OUTSIDE YOURSELF, BEYOND THE ZITS AND CINDERELLA CURFEW. WHEN YOUR GIRLFRIENDS ARE BY YOUR SIDE, YOU CAN MAKE IT THROUGH ANYTHING."
>
> —Amy Fishbein, *The Truth About Girlfriends*

Yes, I know those humanoids with XO chromosomes are the ones who normally spend vacations on golf carts. But thanks to such girlfriends as Mary Lou Retton and Michelle Kwan, we gals can be potential Olympians as well. There are literally hundreds (probably thousands) of women-only learn-to-do-something-athletic retreats.

 **TALKING** ★★★

Sometimes it's more like screaming—for example, when you're careening headfirst down a double black diamond that your ski instructor convinced you to "at least try." But the camaraderie and the we're-in-this-together attitude inspire plenty of meaningful conversations. My sister and I, to this day, still talk (*guffaw* is more like it) about our first ski trip together.

 **GAWKING** ★★★★

In case you haven't heard the statistics, men outnumber women on the ski slopes four to one. Probably even higher on the links. The gawking potential on sports getaways is Rocky Mountain high. They may well deserve an extra star. Four-plus, anyone?

 **ROCKING** ★★★

It depends. Some days you're going to be sore and worn out, and the last thing you'll be up for is highballs around a roaring fire. A hot tub and a pre-news bedtime may be all you can muster. Other times, when you've accomplished big things together, you'll feel like partying all night long. Let's just say that when you're in the mood, the party potential is supreme.

 DOCKING ★★★

Again, it depends. Some sports getaways offer J.Lo–style plush. Others figure you're not in your room anyway, so what's the point? If it's important, check out the brochures ahead of time. Remember to always, always ask questions first.

Not only can you and your girlfriends master golf or skiing or tennis on a girlfriend getaway, but you can also attend a women-only dogsledding camp or women-only avalanche training. At Prophet Muskwa Lodge in British Columbia, you and your girlfriends can learn to light fires with wet matches, to paddle upstream without a paddle (didn't know that was possible, did you?), and to determine whether you should play dead or climb a tree when that bear comes barreling after you. The good news about this five-day training—called the "Complete Girl's Guide to Bush Survival"—is that you only rough it during the day. The rest of the time is spent in first-class accommodations at a world-class spa. You even get daily massages and facials to work out the kinks that inevitably come from climbing trees.

Quite likely, about now you're asking yourself, *Why would I need to learn how to paddle upstream without a paddle?* You probably don't, but what you probably *do* need is a week of amazing scenery, crisp fresh air, and somebody else doing the cooking. The bonding potential on these trips is extreme.

There's No Good Reason to Sit on the Sidelines Anymore

It was fun being a cheerleader and all, but I can't exactly get away with those short skirts and crop tops at my age. Besides, I'd much rather be the one being cheered for.

Which brings up a good point. Girlfriends will cheer for anything. Take golf, for example. No matter how poor my shot off the fifth tee (or sixth tee, or eighteenth tee) might be, girlfriends can always find something about it to cheer. "Well, it went really straight," they might say, neglecting to mention that it only went 30 feet from the tee. If it went really far but landed in the fairway on the next hole over, girlfriends will cheer for the incredible distance of the shot.

Men can't see these things. When we golf with guys, there's always this underlying competition, this need to pretend we're Tiger Woods. Guys want us to play well enough not to embarrass them, but certainly not well enough to beat them. With girlfriends, we're tickled pink at each other's

Half a Dozen or More Surefire Strategies to Ski Free

If your last name is *Pulaski*, if you live in a town named *Pulaski*, or if your name just has a *ski* in it (as in *Roman Polanski*), you could have skied free at Michigan's Indianhead Mountain every March 7 when the resort celebrated the birthday of Revolutionary War hero Casimir Pulaski. Unfortunately, the resort is no longer around.

But it brings up a good point. Free tickets are out there for girlfriends willing to donate canned goods, wear green ski gloves, give up the Super Bowl (quite a sacrifice, I know), or perform other acts of "insanity." Sometimes it's as simple as being in the right place at the right time.

Crested Butte, Colorado, for example, has been known to give out free lift tickets—no strings attached—at various times of the year. Located 230 miles from Denver and a good jaunt from the busy I–70 ski corridor, Crested Butte offers free tickets to attract attention. On Lincoln's birthday Vermont's Sugarbush spotted free tickets to any skier who could recite the entire Gettysburg Address. The point is, keep your ears open.

Here are other strategies for free lift tickets:
1. TURN SEVENTY. Many ski resorts offer complimentary lift tickets to senior citizens with a photo ID.
2. PLAY DUMB. First-time skiers not only pick up free lift tickets but can also land free lessons and equipment rental.
3. FORGET SPRING. If you're willing to continue skiing long after the spring equinox, Maine's Sunday River Resort celebrates Ski Maynia on May 1 with free lift tickets for everyone.
4. PRESIDE OVER ANYTHING. Whether you're the president of the United States, IBM, or the Cedar Rapids Bubble Gum Chewers Association, New Mexico's Sipapu Resort will donate a free lift ticket on Presidents' Day. Just show up with proof of your presidency.

> **5. DONATE CREAMED CORN.** Or any other canned good on January 21, the day Oregon's Mount Bachelor Ski Resort raises money for the homeless and working poor. Called Sharelift Day, the annual charity raises more than 10,000 pounds of food and clothing. Although it's considered poor form to forget the donation, lifts are free to one and all.

success. Which is why learning at a women-only golf or ski or tennis camp is the only way to go.

On women's sports getaways, you don't have to prove yourself or live up to some heroic image. Plus, let's face it, when the men aren't there, you stop worrying if your bathing suit fits or if the sunscreen flatters your complexion—both worries that, when eliminated, make it much easier to relax and learn. To really learn.

Because we girlfriends learn from each other, the model doesn't necessarily have to be "the expert" traversing the double black diamonds. Instead, it can be a fellow camper who's simply learned to stop at the bottom of the hill.

Men also have a hard time being silly when they're playing sports. Women are not above wearing oven mitts on the ski lift or painting a smiling sun around their belly button, something you can have done at Las Olas Surf Safaris (707–746–6435 or www.surflasolas.com), a wonderful women's surfing school near Puerto Vallarta, Mexico (see page 68). Started by Bev Sanders, a totally hip girlfriend who was one of the first to launch snowboarding, Las Olas has one mission: to empower women through surfing.

Which brings up another good point. Many of these women's sports getaways have empowerment as a goal. You don't just learn to ski or find avalanches. You learn to be a better person.

Bev Sanders sees Las Olas as one way she can make a difference in the world. "This world needs strong women. Women are the ones who will stand up for the environment, who will do what needs to be done," she explains. She also hopes to level the playing field. "Look at the ads. Even today, 99 percent of them show men doing the sports," she says. "Where are the women?"

Many of them are starting their own camps and retreats. And when women open a company, especially a learn-to-play-some-sport company, they have a whole different slant. The inner you is every bit as important as the outer athletic ability. Side Trips Retreats for Women, Inc., for example, was started by Peg Schroeder, a yoga instructor whose main mission is to give women the chance to try new things in their life. Try something new here, she reasons, and you can apply it to other areas of your life. Schroeder's company offers golf retreats, Alaskan dogsledding trips, and backpacking excursions on the Appalachian Trail. Leslie Ross, an accomplished telemark skier, created Babes in the Backcountry to share her love of snow with other women.

And not only are our fellow girlfriends opening companies to share what they already know, but many resorts are adding women-only sports packages, as well. These learn-to-fish or learn-to-kayak packages are flying out of marketing directors' computers. What's more, they're tailored specifically for a woman's special abilities, psyche, and strengths. Sometimes the programs even offer child care.

Let's look at a small sampling of women-only sports getaways:

1. *Learn to Ski*. I dare you to find a ski resort anywhere in the world that doesn't offer clinics, camps, and special packages just for women. I guarantee if you call your nearest ski resort, they'll be able to give you a long list of offerings for women only.

Colorado's Winter Park, for example, has a free "Women's Ski Clinic" every year. It starts with breakfast and includes an update on ski gear plus an entire day of ski instruction. Every girlfriend gets a free gift bag, and

> ## Why Girlfriends Make Better Competitors than Guy Friends
>
> 1. They won't pout for five hours when you beat them.
> 2. They understand that how you look in your ski parka [your tennis dress, your golf skirt] is nearly as important as how you play.
> 3. They'll go shopping with you to find a ski parka [tennis dress, golf shirt].
> 4. They won't try to coach you every time you swing a golf club.
> 5. They're willing to discuss the number of fat grams in PowerBars between points.

the sponsors (in one recent year it was Head Skis and Subaru) donate money to the National Breast Cancer Coalition. Call 970–726–1551 for more information.

Winter Park, which is just one of hundreds of ski resorts (there are thirty-five in Colorado alone), also sponsors three-day women's clinics, "Take Your Daughter to the Snow Week," women's weekends, midseason clinics, and W.O.W. (that's "Women of Winter")—a full weekend of tubing, skiing, snowboarding, sleigh riding, and snowshoeing.

If you'd rather learn to telemark, consider a trip to Glenwood Springs. Just 10 miles up Four Mile Road, Sunlight Mountain Resort (970–945–7491 or www.sunlightmtn.com) hosts a three-session telemark series called "In the Company of Women." Taught by an all-women staff of PSIA-certified instructors, these women-only ski sessions are very popular.

2. Learn to Surf. I already mentioned Las Olas (707–746–6435 or www.surflasolas.com). When Bev Sanders was in high school, her dad gave her an office job in his driving school. "Forget college," he said. "Girls don't need an education. What will you do with it once you get married?"

Even though she loved her dad and understood that he was only the product of his generation, Bev quite wisely packed her bags and moved west.

She got a job in Lake Tahoe teaching skiing, a passion she'd had since childhood. That bold move, that decision to abandon old ways of thinking and leap into a new possibility, set the stage for an incredibly big life. Not only did she start one of the first companies to design and manufacture snowboards, but she is also now doing everything within her power to change the way women see themselves—particularly when it comes to sports.

Her current passion, Las Olas, is the premier school for women's surfing. The seven-day programs, best described as a cross between a slumber party and an empowerment seminar, incorporate yoga, massage, and daily surf lessons.

"Women bond in a special way," she says. "I especially love to see these corporate women show up. Within twenty-four hours they're acting like a bunch of monkeys. I always joke that I'm running a reverse finishing school, that I make girls out of women."

Or check out Canada's only all-women surf school. Surf Sister (250–725–4456, 877–724–7873, or www.surfsister.com) introduces women of all ages and abilities to the sport of surfing in a safe, fun, and supportive environment. Surf Sister instructors are friendly, down to earth, and fun to learn from. All instructors are trained in proper surf instruction and emergency first aid.

> *"The idea of combining surf and yoga in a women's retreat was truly life altering! Now, every time I move through Downward Facing Dog into Warrior I am reminded of the rhythm of Mother Ocean and the feminine divine. Surf Sister and Milagro Retreats provided our group of Goddesses with a nurturing, safe environment . . . encouraging our unity with nature."*
>
> —Kathe Faraci, doctor of Traditional Chinese Medicine

3. Learn to Sail. Womanship (800–342–9295 or www.womanship.com), an all-woman sailing school based in Annapolis, Maryland, has sailing schools in San Diego, Florida, the Pacific Northwest, the British Virgin Islands, and the Great Lakes. Since Suzanne Pogell decided to quit her day job in 1984, she has taught more than 25,000 women, ages eighteen to eighty-two, how to sail. Womanship's slogan—"Nobody yells . . . everybody learns"—sums up Pogell's girlfriend-friendly philosophy of relaxed and unintimidating sailing instruction. In addition to the three-, five-, and seven-day live-aboard courses, Pogell offers "Around the World Sail & See Adventures" in Greece, Turkey, New Zealand, Tahiti, Ireland, and the French Riviera.

4. Learn to Ride. Melisa Pearce, a successful coach, Gestalt therapist, and motivational speaker, hosts yearly "Touched by a Horse" events on her Lil Bit North Ranch (303–652–8704 or www.lilbitnorthranch.com) near Boulder, Colorado. And while girlfriends will certainly be able to take on Dale Evans after five days of riding, the main reason for enrolling is to change your life. The seminar includes gourmet meals, professional massage, compelling presentations, and the use of your own mare.

5. *Learn to Mountain Bike.* Dirt Camp (800–711–3478 or www.dirtcamp.com) offers women-only mountain bike camps in Moab, Utah, and Colorado. Designed for riders of all abilities, they're taught by women and include skills drills, single- and double-track rides through spectacular scenery, meals, lodging, and activities.

6. *Learn to Row.* Row As One (617–349–0092 or www.rowasone.org) offers one- to five-day clinics in Boston that help you learn to paddle and work as a team with other crew members.

7. *Learn to Golf.* The retreats at Peg Schroeder's Golf by the Sea (910–397–0907 or www.retreats4women.com) are perfect for girlfriends wanting either to learn to golf or to hone their skills. You stay at Marsh Harbor Inn, a great lodge on semitropical Bald Head Island, North Carolina. You start with yoga, eat gourmet meals, get massages, and of course, play golf with girlfriend golf pros.

8. *Learn to Fly Fish.* Mel Krieger's International School of Fly Fishing in California (800–669–3474 or www.melkrieger.com) offers women-only casting seminars. (Yes, he's a guy, but he has a wife who is just as talented a fisherman as he is.) The three-day seminars include basic casting skills, tackle, entomology, presentation, fly selection, leader construction, and dry-fly and nymphing techniques.

Or make plans to visit the All Women's Fishing Derby at Painter's Lodge in British Columbia (800–663–7090 or www.painterslodge.com). Every June women from all over North America leave behind their busy lives to participate in a four-day weekend of fishing and fun. Sure, great prizes are part of the derby, but it's the lure of camaraderie and friendship that keeps these women coming back year after year. The ladies know they're attending a special event that celebrates and showcases women who want to not only fish, but also prove they can fish and have fun doing it. When you're not on the water, you can take advantage of the many amenities that Painter's Lodge and her sister resort, April Point Resort, have to offer. Experience kayaking, whale-watching, ocean rapids tours, or just relaxing beside the heated outdoor pool.

Five Ego Strokes to Pull Out When You Beat Your Man
(just kidding of course!)

1. "Boy, was I ever lucky today."
2. "Those tips you gave me really helped. I'm not sure what I'd have done without you."
3. "Thanks for letting me win, honey!"
4. "The (a) fifteen beers you drank last night, (b) stress at your office, (c) borrowed tennis racket, or (d) [make up your own excuse for why he lost] sure helped me out today."
5. "I have been modeling my game after you. Looks like it must be working."

True-Life Tales
We're in This Together

THE GIRLFRIENDS:
1. Yours truly, an aging mom who sorta knows how to ski.
2. Jeanine, a New York City writer, also a so-so skier, also "over-the-hill."

THE MISSION:
To learn how to snowboard.

THE DESTINATION:
Sierra-at-Tahoe (530–659–7453 or www.sierratahoe.com), a laid-back resort that, until recently, was family owned and called a ski ranch. Dad plowed the runs, Mom made the snow reports, and the kids taught ski lessons. Although the resort is now owned by a corporation and has ten lifts, 2,000 square feet, and such fancy wizardry as bracelets that open gates and measure your vertical feet, it still has a family feel—something important for all those about to make complete and total fools out of themselves.

THE GETAWAY:
Somewhere between learning to walk and becoming responsible enough to take out the trash, we pick up this infuriating habit called pride. We want to look cool, be applauded, have people say, "Ya know, she's really good at that." Heaven forbid we should try something that makes us look stupid.

    Which is precisely why Jeanine and I chose to take up snowboarding. It would have been much easier to stick with skiing, a sport both of us have more or less mastered. Skiing certainly would have been more statistically correct. The average snowboarder is fifteen, listens to Sprung Monkey, and considers *Wayne's World II* her all-time favorite movie.

But then we compared faces. Adult skiers hesitantly crisscross the mountain with pinched mouths, concentrating on their form. Snowboarders careen down the slopes with wild looks of unadulterated joy. So what if we made complete and utter fools of ourselves? We tossed our ski poles in the trash and whooped, "Like, bring on the embarrassment."

At first we considered wearing a pair of those aviator shades to hide our wrinkles, but finally decided to snowboard as we were— forty-something moms in tight ski pants. Snowboarders wear baggy pants, baggy parkas, and other totally dorky geezer duds. We weren't even sure they'd let us rent boards in our "snowbabe" costumes.

Luckily, the kids in the rental shop were pretty good at keeping a straight face. They even threw in a couple of *you-can-do-its* when I mentioned under my breath that I was a beginner from Kansas.

Jeanine and I decided to make our snowboarding debut at Sierra-at-Tahoe partly because it was so laid back. We began to wonder if they didn't pass out the book *The Seven Habits of Highly Effective People* at employee orientation. The on-mountain photographers give out compliments, the lift operators remind you to smile, and one of the ski instructors dresses up like a priest every year on closing day.

"I give last rites, listen to confessions, and marry anybody who promises to consummate their marriage before they leave the resort," he told us over homemade cookies in the ski lodge.

The other reason we chose Sierra-at-Tahoe for snowboarding goes back to being adults. We thought it would sound "impressive" to say we'd snowboarded there. Sierra-at-Tahoe has the longest half-pipe in America, and Mountain Dew and ESPN do a big snowboarding tour there every year—little trivialities we could throw into any future conversation we might have about the sport.

Needless to say, we weren't asked to join either tour. In fact, our lesson began on a beginner's slope that was flatter than my uncle's wheat field.

Jeanine warned me that our instructor was probably going to be some punk in purple hair who would grunt, "Gnarly, dudette," if we should happen to do anything right. She promised to translate since she'd already taken one lesson from a snowboarder in Vail who abandoned her immediately when he noticed the sixteen-year-old blond twins who were also in the class.

We were pleasantly surprised. Our instructor turned out to be Melodie, a smiling Kelly Preston look-alike. She was thirty-seven, married, and taught school during the off season. Okay, so she did have a bumper sticker on her snowboard that said GIRLS KICK ASS, but she seemed very sympathetic to the class cause. Either that or she was a great actress.

She started with a speech about how this was going to be fun and how we had nothing to be afraid of. She also mentioned that we were spring chickens. Her oldest student has been an eighty-year-old grandma who wanted to "cruise with her grandsons."

She did go on to mention that falling down is part of the fun of snowboarding.

"Whatever you do, don't break your fall with your wrists," she warned us, adding some dire statistics about broken wrists being the number one snowboarding accident. The proper way to fall is by crossing your arms over your chest and letting yourself go. Sometimes, Melodie claimed, this one motion will help you recover and avoid the twenty minutes it takes to gather up all your duds and strap yourself back on the board.

Then she got personal. "Are you goofy or regular?" she asked. Before we could come up with a quick retort—or, for that matter, even the composure to say "duh"—she restated her question. "Which foot is your strongest?" To find out, she gave each of us a rather hefty push on the back. Whichever foot goes forward is allegedly your strong foot. The other way to figure it out is to remember which foot goes first when you do a cartwheel. That's the foot that leads on the snowboard.

Next, we walked around on flat land with a big 5-foot fiberglass board attached to one foot. After a while it began to feel normal.

"Now for the fun stuff," she said with a glimmer in her eye. She reminded me a little of Jack Nicholson in *The Shining*.

But it wasn't that hard. We learned heel turns. Then edge turns. We discovered that when you lean your body just right, the board magically swerves to the right or the left. Of course, we were still on a slope with a three-degree grade.

I was pretty good at heel turns. Jeanine excelled at the edge turns. It was a thrill just to stay up for more than five minutes. Like I said, you have to get over the idea that being sprawled out on the snow with your gear spread around you like a garage sale is embarrassing.

After a couple of hours practicing our turns and, of course, mastering the proper way to fall, Melodie gave us the okay to take the lift.

Getting off the lift was the hardest part. Even though you leave your back foot out, it's quite a feat to jump off a moving chair with a twelve-pound piece of fiberglass stuck to your foot. Naturally Jeanine and I both fell, but we were usually able to scramble off and get out of harm's way. Once I wasn't so lucky and knocked over a nine-year-old boy who was just learning to ski. He was pretty heroic about it, but I feel guilty to this day.

After Melodie ended the class, Jeanine and I went it alone for a few runs. We got a good laugh about Melodie going back to the lodge and guffawing with her husband, also a snowboard teacher, about the two antiques she'd taught.

Perhaps that best sums up our snowboarding experience. Lots of laughs. Lots of falls. Lots of looking like complete idiots.

But you know what? We tried something that most people our age will never do. So what if I lost my sunglasses? So what if the bruise on my right cheek (and I don't mean the cheek on my face) took three weeks to heal? We tried it. And while neither of us conquered the snowboard, we conquered something more important—our fear of appearing foolish.

We also bonded in a whole new way. Like soldiers who battle side by side in war, Jeanine and I felt closer as we helped each other to our feet, cheered each other on. We e-mail each other to this day.

On our last run up the mountain, we even got off the lift without falling. We looked at each other with a big smile, gave each other the high five, and said, "Gnarly, dude."

• • • • • • • • • • • • • • • • •

Sisters in the Steeps

THE GIRLFRIENDS:
1. Mary, a former Outward Bound instructor and current Pilates instructor from Boulder, Colorado.
2. Fourteen other die-hard backcountry babes.

THE MISSION:
To improve backcountry and avalanche skills.

THE DESTINATION:
"A Women's Ski and Avalanche Weekend Workshop" with Babes in the Backcountry (970–453–4060 or www.babesinthebackcountry.com) on Silverton Mountain in the San Juan Mountains of Colorado.

THE GETAWAY (as told by Mary):
"I almost bailed on "Sisters in the Steeps." The workshop fell in the driest Colorado April since 1968. Word on the street said the backcountry was melting ruthlessly. What's more, the hosting ski area, Silverton Mountain, huddled in the precipitous San Juans, did not lend itself to the fake-it-till-you-make-it skier. Silverton Mountain heralds tight chutes and a dearth of moderate terrain. Most of all, I was catching cold feet at the notion of embarking on an adventure with fifteen felines. This was a new paradigm for me, unfamiliar and

scary. But with a little yoga and positive thought, I committed to doing my best and prayed that the sisters would accept me.

"In spite of my hesitation, I found myself in a room full of fit and enthusiastic women hoping to 'improve decision making' and 'gain confidence,' under the tutelage of our instructors: seasoned female telemark skiers, pro snowboarders, and avalanche forecasters. The group felt welcoming and motivated. We had already doubled the female population of Silverton, Colorado.

"After searching for avalanche beacons in the parking lot, the Avalung, the renovated 1972 chairlift, whisked us up 1,900 feet to a pass aloft the Colorado Basin. There we dismounted our boards and hiked a ridge to the top of an avalanche gully called the Colorado Run. One of our instructors offered advice and caution, then immediately pointed her board down the fall line. At once, I was enveloped in a descending sea of aggressive and graceful women.

"The force of these women diving into gravity's arms warmed my cold feet. There was a power in this group that I hadn't experienced in mixed company. It was as if the lack of gender barriers urged us to enhance our strengths and breathe through our weaknesses. Inspired by this rush of raw spirit, I began to kick my own buttocks, just so I could strive to match the sisters. Informed decisions were made, and variable conditions were negotiated. By the afternoon we were a unified band of babes, hiking up an exposed and corniced ridge.

"After passing up our destination couloir due to a steep entrance and a setting sun, we chose a serpentine col that emptied into a bowl of pristine snow. One at a time we picked our way through the stripe of white, bracketed by alpine rock. Soon the wave of women were together again laughing, sharing Scoobie snacks, and telling stories.

"At the end of this first day, I asked another sister what seemed different about hanging in the backcountry with a bunch of women. She looked at me, smiled, and said, 'The boys would have gone down that first chute.'"

—*Thanks to Mary Laurence-Bevington for providing this True-Life Tale.*

Road Trips

Move Over, Thelma and Louise!

> **"DESPITE WHAT YOU'VE SEEN IN THE MOVIES, YOU DON'T HAVE TO KILL A MAN TO GO ON A ROAD TRIP. JUST WANTING TO KILL SOMEONE IS ENOUGH."**
>
> —Cameron Tuttle, *The Bad Girl's Guide to the Open Road*

Road trips are impromptu getaways taken in a car. Unlike Sunday drives or family vacations, road trips are done for no other purpose than to flaunt your nose at convention. Suitcases? Fagetaboutit. Itinerary? What's that? Destination? We'll know when we get there.

Road trips can happen spontaneously. You're on your way to pick out wallpaper for the spare guest room and you decide to go to Winslow, Arizona, instead. Or you're heading to work and you turn left when right goes straight to corporate headquarters. The fact that you have a girlfriend who not only cheers you on in this anomalous reversal, but also adds, "I'll go with you," says a lot about a girlfriend's character.

 **TALKING:** ★★★★

Maybe we should even throw in an extra star for this category. Even if for some strange unforeseen reason you didn't want to talk (unheard of, I know), there's little other choice when you're encased in a capsule that averages eight feet by fifteen.

 **GAWKING:** ★★★★

Think Brad Pitt in the film *Thelma and Louise*. In fact, road trips are your big chance to get the Brad Pitts of the world before the Jennifer Anistons of the world marry them. When Brad played J. D., the hitchhiker Thelma managed to pick up, he was a veritable nobody. The point is, you can be pretty sure that hitchhikers haven't made it yet. It's your opportunity to get them on the way up.

I'd be remiss if I didn't mention that there is one slight drawback. Sometimes these hunky hitchhikers have professions such as serial killer or bank robber. That's why we savvy girlfriends always leave room in the trunk. That way, after we boink said hitchhikers over the head with coolers and tie their wrists and legs with jumper cables, we have a place to stash them until we can get to a police station.

 **ROCKING:** ★★★★

The rules of a road trip are pretty simple. (1) No one from home will ever know. (2) The people you meet will never see you again. Did someone say, "Rock on!"

 DOCKING:

Accommodations on a road trip often suck sewer slime. There is that rare occasion when you get invited to some lavish company cocktail party and end up passing out in the suite where it was held, but for the most part road trips do not excel in comfy accommodations.

These sorts of road trips usually happen without conscious awareness. One morning you're daintily sipping coffee laced with Sweet'N Low, and the next thing you know you're swilling margaritas with a drunken cowboy named Marvin.

You, as responsible, Day-Timer-following citizens, had no way of knowing it was going to happen. There's rarely a warning. Premeditation wasn't involved. For all intents and purposes you are justified in pleading innocent. You didn't intentionally forget to tell anyone. You just plain and simple didn't see it coming. Blame it on your inner diva, that great adventurous goddess of inner wisdom, who knew it was high time to say bye-bye, sayonara, later-tater to the monotonous old rut.

When it comes right down to it, that's what road trips are all about. Crashing out of the box. I mean, c'mon, who really needs clean underwear every day or prescheduled trips to the health club? What's the higher purpose in keeping track of Weight Watcher points, stalking sales at Macy's, and getting up every morning to the chalk-on-a-blackboard screech of an alarm clock?

With road trips, you (and your girlfriends) are on your own. No one needs *you* to find his science homework or wash the basketball jersey that's been stuffed under *her* pillow for the last week and a half. No one cares if your hair is clean or your lipstick matches your purse. There's no clock, no guidelines, no titles.

On a road trip, in fact, you can pick your own title. You get to be a "babe" or a "gypsy" or even a "loose woman." The point is: You get to choose.

Unless you make it onto one of those MOST WANTED posters (and of course there's no guarantee that won't happen), you can pretty much count on complete and total anonymity on a road trip.

Which brings up a good point. Road trips can save you big bucks on therapy. In case you haven't checked lately, therapy rings in at roughly a hundred dollars an hour. On a road trip therapy is completely free. You can discuss the finer points of your dysfunctional family with the drunk slumped over his gin tonic for as long as you want. He's not going to tell you "time's up" or ask you to redefine what you meant by that last statement. Even if he could remember what you said, he'd never dare breathe a word of it to anyone. Course, if he did, you'd be traveling light in the next state over by then.

It's only fair to warn you: The total freedom that road trips bring can take a while. We're still women, after all. The first few hours can sometimes entail guilt. You're tempted to call the answering machine, to check in with your secretary, to make sure little Susie made it to piano lessons. But just know that within a few hours on the road, you'll notice your heels spontaneously tapping to Aretha Franklin's "R-E-S-P-E-C-T." Before you can say *Route 66* a hundred times, you'll be smiling, enjoying the strands of hair the wind is whipping onto your face. You'll be belting out Cyndi Lauper's "Girls Just Want to Have Fun" and scrambling to remember the date of your firstborn's birthday.

The main word to remember is *Just do it.* Okay, so it's three words. Who's counting? Anything you've ever fantasized about is fair game. What? You're still worrying about your regular routine? Tear off that noose right now. Throw off that yoke! Let it go, girl!

Before Heading Off into the Sunset

As I mentioned, it sometimes takes a bit of pavement between home and the open road before fully allowing yourself to scream, "Screw it!" Thelma, after all, was still combing her hair three full days after murdering her dance partner. As women, we just have to accept the fact that some of us need a "plan" before peeling out of the driveway. This section is for you. It contains all the lugnuts and deadbolts of planning your girlfriend road trip getaway.

How Many Girlfriends Does It Take to Fill Up a Phone Booth or, in This Case, a Pink Cadillac?

One best girlfriend is enough for a road trip. Particularly if she has an impressive credit line on her Visa card. But two girlfriends or even three brings variety to the party. More than four makes it hard to pick up those Brad Pitt look-alikes who will inevitably be lining the highway.

While discretion is not the goal of a road trip getaway, keep in mind that you will, whether you already are or not, be bonded with these girlfriends for life.

And always remember solo road trips work, too.

Your Wheels or Mine?

Not everybody has a baby blue 1966 Thunderbird convertible, the car Thelma and Louise drove off into obscurity. That's okay. The main thing to take into consideration is that your getaway car should move. And it should at least have an AM radio.

World's Best Road Songs

If you're lucky and your roadmobile has more than an AM radio (maybe even a CD player?), here's a not-very-comprehensive list of tunes for the road:

1. "All I Wanna Do Is Have Some Fun," Sheryl Crow.
2. "Express Yourself," Madonna.
3. "Bad Girls," Donna Summer.
4. "Girls Just Wanna Have Fun," Cyndi Lauper.
5. "On the Road Again," Willie Nelson.
6. "Celebration," Kool and the Gang.

Despite all advice to the contrary, in the case of getaway cars, size *does* matter. Let's say one of you has a 1986 Ford Escort. Nancy Reagan, whom I hasten to add wouldn't be caught dead on a girlfriend road trip, did have one piece of sage advice: Just say no! The bigger, the boatier, the better. If all else fails (which means all your girlfriends drive '86 Ford Escorts), consider tying beer cans (empty ones, of course; the full ones should be kept on ice in the front seat) to the back bumper, or borrowing some of your boyfriend's shaving cream.

The ultimate road trip car is an art car such as Nicole Goldman's "Twinkle, Twinkle Little Car," a 1992 Honda Civic that's covered completely with 200 software CDs, or Tom Kennedy's "Ripper the Friendly Shark," a 1982 Nissan with a fin on top and rubber fish hanging from its ceiling. Barring the hijacking of an official art car, you can always write

O-E-BABY with ketchup on your automobile. Whatever you do, don't try mustard. It strips the paint.

It also helps if your getaway car has a full tank of gas. And of course the number one, don't-even-think-about-forgetting-this part is, your roadmobile has to have a name. Something like Big Brutus. Or the Partymobile.

To Pack or Not to Pack

Don't bring anything you'd hate to see blow out the window. The less you pack, the better. Think *thrift stores.* And not the ones in the hometown you're leaving. Even dinky towns like Ark City, Kansas, have secondhand stores where you can replenish your wardrobe. The only musthaves are a hat, a pair of sunglasses, a driver's license, and a credit card that is not maxed out.

Whatever you do, leave these things at home: photos of family members, lipstick, fashion magazines, blow dryers, your wedding ring, miscellaneous small children.

Bring the cell phone if you must, but leave it turned off in the glove box except in dire emergencies such as tracking down the name of the cute guy driving license plate 56789–82.

Underwear Tag and Other Sports to Take Up on the Road

After you've discussed every conceivable guy you've ever dated, ever married, ever made love to, and ever wanted to make love to, there may be some free time. Just maybe. In the rare instance that this should happen, here are five road games to keep you occupied.

1. **JUMPER CABLE JUMP ROPE.** You take one end. Girlfriend No. 2 takes the other, and Girlfriend No. 3 jumps to her heart's content.
2. **UNDERWEAR TAG.** After three days of wearing the same pair of underwear, you're probably going to want to dispose of it. Laundry detergent, after all, does have limitations. Throwing them out the car window in strategic locations is very effective at luring in testosterone-style help. It's particularly useful in getting flats fixed, oil changed, and belts lubed. Need I say more?
3. **ROADKILL COLLECTING.** Masters at this game might even collect enough to make a fur coat souvenir by the end of the trip.
4. **LICENSE PLATE GAME.** Yeah, yeah, yeah, you already know this one. In the girlfriend getaway version, you find a license plate and then tell a story about someone you know with ties from that state. For example, Pennsylvania: You were once engaged to a guy who sold door-to-door blow-up dolls in Erie.
5. **ALPHABET GAME.** First you find the letter (on a bumper sticker, a road sign, a license plate, wherever), and then you relate a fantasy that starts with that letter. For example, *M:* I've always wanted to have a personal maid.

Which Direction to Point the Steering Wheel

Again, you don't need advice from any book. By far the best strategy is to begin driving and see where you end up. But in memory of Elaine Googlemyer, a third-grade classmate who refused to pick up a pencil without the teacher telling her how to do it, here are some suggestions:

1. Gravestones of famous women (see the sidebar on page 144 for specific suggestions).
2. Cities from your favorite movies.
3. Places you've seen on postcards.
4. Wacky museums, food festivals, and unknown landmarks—say, the world's largest ball of string.
5. Kansas.

Important Things to Practice Before You Go

Hopefully, you're already well versed at such necessities as creative peeing (usually by the side of the road), gearshift cuddling (for those nights when your leaky pocketbook mandates sleeping in the car), and shameless racking (done with your knee when perfect strangers start to become more strange). But there are still a few other things that every road-tripping girlfriend would be wise to practice before opening the throttle.

1. Calling "shotgun." Best done in a loud, persuasive voice, this yodel will, of course, ensure your rightful spot in the front seat.

2. Sign language. Important for communicating with attractive strangers in BMWs.

3. Believable excuses. These work well with police officers with red lights on their cars.

4. Fancy leg poses. In case your car breaks down and you forgot to bring a lug wrench.

5. Fountain diving. Yes, for pocket change that charitable types have thrown into fountains for the local children's hospital. This should be done under no circumstances unless you're totally desperate and then, of course, you must make a solemn vow to yourself that you'll send a check with double the amount back when you're home and rolling in dough again.

For those of you who haven't gotten it yet, here's an official permission slip that you can tear out, stick in your wallet, give to your boss, or use for covering private parts if the police should happen to get involved.

Permission Slip

To Whom It May Concern:

_____[fill in your name here]_____

has unconditional, undivided, unmitigated permission to do whatever she wants. She gets to decide where she's going, what she's going to do when she gets there, and how she's going to do it. So there.

Signed,
Phineas T. Grout

True-Life Tales
Fine Dining at Chevron

THE GIRLFRIENDS:
1. Mary, a forty-something PR executive.
2. Pam, an artist whose sister is Mary's veterinarian.

THE MISSION:
To laugh. The kids were gone and the girlfriends, who had suffered recent relationship setbacks, needed to have some fun.

THE DESTINATION:
San Luis Obispo, California, two hours up the coast, site of a former memorable girlfriend getaway.

THE GETAWAY *(as told by Mary)*:
"My friend Pam and I were broke but determined to go have fun while our kids were visiting family. We decided on a Thelma and Louise theme and took her BMW convertible up the coast to San Luis Obispo. We dug out our vintage scarves and sunglasses, donned bright red lipstick, and struck out after work one Friday. With the top down, we smiled and waved at almost every car we passed.

"Since our credit cards were maxed out, except for a gas credit card, we decided all meals and necessities would have to be purchased at Chevron gas stations. (That meant eating nachos, hot dogs, and honey buns for the entire trip.)

"We took a Polaroid camera and captured memories at these stops. The employees thought we were crazy.

"After a night of dancing and clubbing with men young enough to be our . . . um, younger brothers . . . we discovered there was some big deal in San Luis Obispo that booked every possible room at every single hotel in town. We drove around and around until we ended up in Shell Beach. The ritzy beachfront hotel there had a cancellation after 2:00 A.M., and we were able to negotiate a good rate. With that expenditure tapping us of all our resources, we ended up spending the following night in the car.

"We spent our days on the beach (even visiting the topless beach at Avila!), our evenings dancing, and had the most fun anyone could imagine!"

World's Cheesiest Pickup Lines

(submitted by Vicki Salemi)

1. "I make great omelets for breakfast."
2. "Let's not bother your friends, they're having fun."
3. "Let's go check out your car."
4. "It's my birthday, kiss me."
5. "Your hair is interesting. It's like vines."

Hasta la Vista, Baby

THE GIRLFRIENDS:
1. April, a Boulder (Colorado) defense attorney.
2. Linda Sue, a Boulder defense attorney.
3. Gayle, a Boulder prosecuting attorney.

THE MISSION:
To escape real life.

THE DESTINATION:
Santa Fe or Bust.

THE GETAWAY:
Gayle's brother was visiting Colorado from England. Not only did he have a wife with a title and a couple of mistresses back home, but he immediately began hitting on future mistresses in Boulder. Gayle had been dealing with him all week and finally told her husband, "You know, I can't handle him anymore. I'm leaving." She called Linda Sue (who was going through a divorce) and April (whose twenty-two- and twenty-four-year-old kids were driving her crazy) and said, "We need to get out of town." Since the three women had already traveled together (to Boston with husbands in tow, to a B&B that Linda Sue owns off the coast of Venezuela, on a biking trip from Boulder to Santa Fe), they knew they'd have fun.

With no clue where they'd stay (Santa Fe in October can be busy; who knew if they'd find a room?), they loaded up Gayle's blue Audi that they named "The Marquis de Sade" and headed south with lots of country-and-western music in the CD player. They did find rooms, although they had to stay at two different hotels, did some power shopping, and came back with a whole new take on their problems.

• • • • • • • • • • • • • • • • •

Eight New and Improved Uses for a Day-Timer

The best possible use for a Day-Timer is to shred it into confetti that you'll throw out the window as you head for the highway. If Lady Bird Johnson's admonitions not to litter are still stored in your memory bank, you're free to try these other uses for a Day-Timer:

1. **QUASI-TABLE.** Great for balancing burgers, fries, and malts while maneuvering around eighteen-wheelers.

2. **MATCHMAKER.** Write your phone number on leftover blank pages and pass them out to interesting-looking strangers at truck stops, burger joints, and gas stations.

3. **ART PROJECTS.** The pages fold nicely into origami swans and peacocks.

4. **ATTENTION GETTERS.** You can beat them against the dash of the car if fellow girlfriends get whiny.

5. **TOILET PAPER.** The pages with next month's itinerary are particularly satisfying to use in a pinch.

6. **EXHAUST-PIPE STUFFERS.** If one of those guys you gave your phone number to starts morphing into Thelma's Harlan (you remember, the guy in the parking lot), you can take the Day-Timer, stuff it in his exhaust pipe, and burn rubber.

7. **DIPSTICK WIPER.** You're probably not going to be checking your oil that often, but if the car starts smoking or something, you won't have to scramble around for a paper towel.

8. **KINDLING FOR CAMPFIRES.**

Celebration Getaways

How to Make a Wedding Shower Last Four Days

> **"OUR LIVES WOULD BE A FUZZY DASH FROM ONE OBLIGATION TO ANOTHER IF WE DIDN'T PAUSE MOMENTARILY AND MARK OUR ACCOMPLISHMENTS, EXPLORE OUR CHALLENGES, AND SHARE OUR DAY-TO-DAY CIRCUMSTANCES WITH OUR GIRLFRIENDS."**
>
> —Carmen Renee Berry, Tamara Traeder, and Janet Hazen,
> *Girlfriends: Invisible Bonds, Enduring Ties*

It's not news to anybody that celebrations demand girlfriends. Whether we're toasting a new job, knitting booties for our sister's twins, or preparing to launch a marriage, we need girlfriends to handle the important details. Like food, guest lists, and wrapping paper.

 **TALKING** ★★★★

Think nostalgia. Think happy memories. Think of every fun event you haven't talked about (let alone thought about) in ten years.

 GAWKING ★–★★★★

Since there's an awful lot of leeway in celebration getaways, it's clearly difficult to rate. If you're celebrating your birthday in Juneau, Alaska (which happens to have the highest ratio of single men to women in this country), the scenery will be stupendous. If, on the other hand, you're celebrating the impending birth of triplets on a girls-only fishing trip, well, sorry, you're on your own.

 **ROCKING** ★★★★

Does the word *celebration* ring any bells? Let's pop open that champagne.

 **DOCKING** ★–★★★★

Hmm. Like the gawking factor, the docking factor on celebration getaways is pretty nebulous. You are certainly free to pick out a five-star hotel (and why not, if you can afford it?), but even if the trees in your yard don't grow money, you can have a real blast at Motel 6.

Guys are great for checking on scores and stock prices, but they leave a lot to be desired in the planning and preparation department. Left to their masculine devices, our most treasured moments would revolve around day-old store-bought cakes, gifts of vacuum cleaners, and maybe a rushed meal at Denny's.

Girlfriends, on the other hand, instinctively know how to throw a bash, how to mark our special accomplishments with gusto, how to say "you go, girl!" in a zesty way. That part's a given and doesn't need a chapter in a getaway book.

But what if . . . what if we took the celebration one step further? What if, instead of celebrating our birthdays, our new children, our upcoming weddings, our new jobs in the customary way, we celebrated them by getting out of town, by shutting out everything else and putting our attention on that great therapist in the sky—in the form of our girlfriends?

Of course we'll still give gifts, but wow! Why not have the Eiffel Tower—or Bloomingdale's, for that matter—in the background of your photos?

The great thing about a celebration getaway is it can be any one of the other types of getaways—it can be a spa getaway to celebrate your birthday, a learn-to-surf getaway to celebrate your new job, a spiritual getaway to celebrate your new wisdom in a new decade. A celebration getaway can be almost anything. There are, however, five rules:

1. You must put on your thinking cap and try something creative.
Seeing an ad in a newspaper travel section might be exciting, but why not come up with your own package tours of your own historic sites? Maybe you'll want to visit the graves of famous women. Or throw a Bette Davis film fest in Solano. Or take a tour of the birthday girl's former homes.

2. You must take a camera. For years Carol was the documentarian of our getaways. No matter how negligent the rest of us were ("I just ran out of film," "Ah shucks, the camera's in the shop," et cetera), Carol was always there with her trusty Minolta. She'd take pictures, make copies of each one, and dutifully mail them off to the rest of us. Until Carol finally got it: Girlfriend getaways, above all else, are meant to be low on stress and high on relaxation. She finally resigned from her job as camerawoman. Now all of us remember to bring cameras.

Celebrations with Chutzpah

"When your bridesmaids end up in the Jacuzzi with their dresses on, it's a good party."

—Emily Robison, Dixie Chick

3. You must bring pictures. Pictures from past get-aways are perfect. But so are pictures of children, former husbands, favorite pets, and new homes.

4. Bring "remember when" stories—especially about the person who is being honored. You can even bring props, such as that embarrassing green face mask stuff your friend was wearing the first time you met, in the college dorm bathroom. When we recall special memories, it binds us together, makes our friendship stronger.

5. Bring papers and pen. When my friends threw a baby shower for me, they each wrote a short letter to my daughter, Tasman, on the tablecloth. They told stories about her mom (that's me) and passed on wishes and dreams for her life. I can tell you that even though that tablecloth was paper, it will never make it to the trash can.

Five Shower Gifts That Will Never Make It Through Airport Security

1. Designer knife block.
2. Pearl-handled cheese knife.
3. Melon baller.
4. Easy Spackle-Splice and Dice-O-Matic.
5. Custom-made shotgun.

Twenty Celebrations That Call for a Girlfriend Getaway

My friend Kitty and I always trade cards on our anniversary. Of course, it's an easy date to remember: We met on Valentine's Day 1979 at the Overland Park, Kansas, Ramada Inn where she was a hostess and I was a sales rep.

If you're looking for an excuse to launch a girlfriend getaway celebration, look no further than this list of twenty:

1. Birthdays.
2. Impending marriages.
3. Divorces.
4. Second impending marriages.
5. Mother's Day.
6. Anniversary of the day you met.
7. Hina-Matsuri, a Japanese holiday for girls (March 3).
8. Lucille Ball's birthday (August 6).
9. PMS parties.
10. Release date of *Thelma and Louise* (November 11).
11. Roman Festival of Peace honoring Roman goddess Pax (January 30).
12. Women's Merrymaking Day (November 25).
13. Day of Mawu, the African creator goddess (November 30).
14. Children's birthdays (or the anniversary of the day *you* gave birth).
15. Wives Feast in Ireland (February 1).
16. The day Jane Addams, president of the International League for Peace and Freedom, won the Nobel Peace Prize (December 10).
17. The day Janet Reno became the first woman U.S. attorney general (March 12).
18. Woman's Equality Day, when the states ratified women's suffrage (aka the Nineteenth Amendment to the U.S. Constitution).
19. Third impending marriages.
20. Anniversary of Sally Ride becoming America's first woman astronaut (June 18).

True-Life Tales
When Time Stood Still

THE GIRLFRIENDS:
1. Susan, tourist and convention director for the Del Rio, Texas, Chamber of Commerce.
2. Her friends from the birthday club—Olga, Almeda, Trish, Enriqueta, and Agnes.

THE MISSION:
To celebrate Susan's fortieth birthday.

THE DESTINATION:
Inn on the Creek in Del Rio (since washed away by the worst flood in that city's history).

THE GETAWAY *(as told by Susan):*
"On my forty-something birthday, my birthday club friends gave me a special present, the gift of time. We went to the Inn on the Creek in Del Rio and took full advantage of the break in daily life.

"We walked by San Felipe Creek and listened to its gentle ripple; we sat in the hot tub, looking over the fluttering green leaves of the pecan trees and sparkle of the creek, and talked about our children and our lives.

"I was a reporter, stressed, divorced, with a teenage daughter. I was floundering. I told my friends about the man I was seeing, now my husband, and we drank champagne as we soaked away the strain of daily living. Later we sat on the patio, devoured a candlelight dinner of salmon, fresh fruit, and shrimp, and talked some more.

"It was a perfect birthday.

"Since that birthday, many things have changed. One of my friends lost her son last year; one friend's daughter ran away from home and is now living with a man her mother despises. Children are married or working on their master's degrees. But my birthday club still meets when we find time. The worst flood in Del Rio history washed the inn away, but not our memories, and not before I spent my honeymoon and first anniversary there. That last time I bought a sunflower table in the inn. It sits in my living room. Every time I see it, I remember my birthday gathering with friends, and the start of a close-enough-to-perfect life.

"The table could now be driftwood, and I could be the same. I think of the place where time stood still for a little while, just long enough for me to catch my breath and continue my upstream journey."

—*Thanks to Susan Leonard-Cottle for providing this True-Life Tale.*

• • • • • • • • • • • • • • • •

Viva Las Vegas

THE GIRLFRIENDS:
1. Jennifer, mother of two, from Washington, D.C.
2. Cindy, her best friend, a clinical researcher in New York.
3. Tina, a friend from Los Angeles.

THE MISSION:
Do Vegas in twenty-four hours.

THE DESTINATION:
The Venetian Hotel (877–857–1861 or www.venetian.com) in Las Vegas. Not only does this hotel feature accurate near-scale replicas of Venice's most famous landmarks, but there's an indoor canal complete with gondolas and singing gondoliers. If that weren't enough, this over-the-top lodging also boasts seventeen specialty

restaurants, fifty boutiques, two museums—a branch of the Guggenheim and one of Madame Tussaud's Wax Museum—and the largest hotel rooms (*Guinness* even confirms this) in the world.

THE GETAWAY *(as told by Jennifer):*

"My best friend, Cindy, called me the afternoon the September 2000 issue of *Essence* was delivered to her doorstep. 'Have you looked at the new *Essence* yet?' No, I don't have it. 'Wait until you see it. They have a feature on Lela Rochon and Vanessa Bell Calloway doing Vegas in twenty-four hours. It looks so live! Check it out, because that's what I want to do for my birthday.'

"Naturally, I was intrigued. We'd traveled together in the past and had created some awesome memories on those trips. Most notably, renting a cabin in the Georgia mountains with three other friends for our twenty-fourth and twenty-fifty birthdays.

"I ran to the nearest store and picked up the magazine. There, on page 196, were Lela and Vanessa chillin' on a gondola in the Venetian Hotel, talking about the luxurious spa services at the Canyon Ranch SpaClub, and doing what we women seem to do best—shop. The moment I got home, I called Cindy and told her to count me in!

"Fast-forward two months.

"I departed from D.C. to Atlanta only to learn that the connecting flights to Vegas were overbooked, and my only hope of making the trip was to fly into L.A. and drive with our girlfriend Tina (who happened to live there). So that's what I did. And even though that might seem a bit extreme for a twenty-four-hour trip, we had the best time on that four-hour car ride. Cindy was waiting for us at the Venetian, having flown effortlessly from Atlanta. Our whirlwind weekend began.

"The three of us squealed with delight as we reunited and admired the luxurious suite we were staying in—even grander than we imagined, with a bathroom the size of a small New York apartment outfitted with more marble than the Metropolitan Museum of Art.

"After resting for a few hours, it was time to hit the town. First stop, Postrio, Wolfgang Puck's delightful restaurant. I can taste my lobster risotto to this day, and we're not going to even talk about the crème brûlée. We sat in the dark corner for hours, sipping wine, planning our lives, and doling out advice. After dinner we walked around the Venetian in amazement. It was like a small Italian town. Every store you could imagine, from Jimmy Choo to BCBG Max Azria—a woman's paradise here on earth.

"The next morning we woke up bright and early and headed to the Canyon Ranch SpaClub—also located in the hotel (what wasn't?). A wholesome breakfast was served, followed by spa services. The spa itself was spectacular, and from the moment we wrapped our brown bodies in those terry-cloth robes we felt completely transformed. One by one attendants appeared, called our names, and escorted us to the back for the most luxurious spa treatments imaginable.

"By the time we left the spa we were famished. Already squeaky clean and moist from showering and using every Philosophy product they had, we headed back to our room to change and head out for lunch at P. F. Chang's. We dined for hours. And I must admit, there's nothing like a nice glass of wine, trying superb new appetizers, and dishing with the girls. Had we stayed any longer, dinner would have been served.

"In a relaxed and happy mood, we practically walked all the way back to our hotel (we had caught a cab to the restaurant) by way of every other hotel on the Strip. There was a unanimous agreement: Ours was the best. We walked into so many shops that our feet were pleading for mercy. But that didn't stop us from a quick try at the slot machine. Three quarters each. Who came to Vegas to lose money? Last, a quick stop at Sephora.

"We headed back to the room to rest before dinner and an evening with Joe Sample at the Blue Note. As we got ready for a night on the town, we laughed and filled each other in on the latest and best beauty products. We exited the hotel picture perfect and into the wrong cab, which drove us around in circles and dropped us off so far away from our venue we practically crawled to the Blue Note (cute feet aren't always comfortable feet), only to discover we'd missed half the show. Oh well, we couldn't let that ruin our trip. So we settled on the nearest restaurant for dinner, a cute little bistro that served an array of yummy entrees. More wine, laughter, support, and mapping out our lives, and then it was time to head back home.

"We rushed back to the Venetian, where I grabbed my bags (already packed and waiting by the door), and Tina and Cindy whisked me off to the airport for my midnight flight. I made it. Completely exhausted. Completely satisfied. And already thinking about the next time I would be able to get away with the girls—even if only for twenty-four hours."

—Thanks to Jennifer Ransaw Smith for providing this True-Life Tale.

• • • • • • • • • • • • • • • • •

Fifty Years and Counting

THE GIRLFRIENDS:
1. Marilyn, a just-retired flight attendant with United Airlines.
2. Linda, a preschool teacher.
3. Diane, a social worker.
4. Ellyn, an attorney.
5. Cathy, an actuary.
6. Roseann, a realtor and country club hostess.

THE MISSION:
To celebrate all six of their sixtieth birthdays.

THE DESTINATION:
Roseann's favorite place—Palm Island Resort in Cape Haze, Florida (800–824–5412 or www.palmisland.com). Palm Island—you have to take a ferry to get there—has one-, two-, and three-bedroom

villas right on the Gulf of Mexico. It also has screened-in porches for sunset viewing, four swimming pools, eleven tennis courts, a resident pirate named Red Beard, a seafood restaurant, and water sports and nature/recreation programs for all ages.

THE GETAWAY:

These six friends have known each other since third grade. They have faithfully attended every one of their high school reunions as a team, and a few years ago decided to "get away" together. They started with a lake home in Eagle River, Wisconsin, and have been planning trips together ever since. Although most of them still live in the Chicago area (they grew up in Franklin Park), their getaways are special times to talk, as Marilyn says, "until their jaws get tired."

They eat a lot (and frequently pick places with kitchens so they can cook), jitterbug, and reminisce about fifty-plus years of friendship. They bring wine, snacks, and all sorts of photos of husbands, children, grandchildren, and special events.

"It's almost like we regress to our school days. We become a bunch of silly girls. We still love to talk about high school and old boyfriends and the first time we got kissed," says Marilyn, who keeps a diary complete with photos of the friends' many years together.

"I can't always remember what I did yesterday, but I remember these memories from high school," she adds.

The remote Palm Island was perfect for their sixtieth celebration. Topping off the weekend was an encounter in a nearby restaurant, where the Silver Girls (as they sometimes call themselves) happened upon a bachelor party of twenty-something young men. The groom-to-be, possibly having had too many drinks, stumbled up to them and asked with a disappointed look on his face, "Are you the girls we hired?"

• • • • • • • • • • • • • • • • •

Spiritual Getaways

The Closest Thing to Heaven for Now

> **"I COULD HAVE PRAYED ALONE, BUT I DIDN'T WANT TO. I WANTED COMPANY AND SUPPORT AND INTIMACY."**
>
> —Nina Wise, *A Big New Free Happy Unusual Life*

One could argue that in some ways any girlfriend getaway could qualify as a spiritual getaway. By its very nature, a getaway with your girlfriends refreshes you spiritually. There's something about being with your buds that forces you back to center, that brings you back to what's really important. It's a guarantee practically written into the contract: You're going to come back renewed and more balanced, even if your getaway is spent at the craps table in Reno, Nevada.

TALKING: ★★

This may be the only type of girlfriend getaway where talking isn't why you're there. In fact, chatting of any kind—especially in sanctuary hallways or a chapel—is often frowned upon. Nonetheless, you *will* be communicating with your girlfriends—in a whole new way—a more wordless, deeper way. Perhaps in this chapter I should change the criterion from talking to communing—and in that case spiritual getaways would get four big stars.

 **GAWKING:**

For once you are not going to be thinking about men . . . unless, of course, you still think of the big guy upstairs as a "he." The only humanoid men you are likely to come across are monks in brown robes, *celibate* monks in brown robes, so don't expect much in the scenery department.

 **ROCKING:** ★★

I am giving this category a couple of stars because rocking your soul is important business. You won't be rocking your bootie, of course. In fact, you'll probably be ignoring your bootie altogether. After all, you are here to nurture your spirit, your soul, that part of you that has better things to do than put on makeup. And when it comes right down to it, that's who you really are anyway.

 DOCKING: ★★

Again, the number of stars is misleading. Most spiritual getaways don't have material comfort as their number one mission. Get over it. Instead of nurturing your bratty inner child, you will be nurturing your soul. At a spiritual getaway, you can find everything from exquisite tropical gardens to simple cabins heated only by a woodstove. But boy, the beauty you find inside!

But in this chapter we're going to discuss intentional spiritual getaways, getaways that take your spirituality one step farther, where you go to meditate or sit in the silence or to learn how to live by the principles of, say, the ancient goddess of Crete.

At some time or another, you probably visited a cathedral or a famous church. Maybe it was in sixth grade on a field trip. Or when you went to Amsterdam back in college on that Eurail pass. That is not the kind of spiritual getaway we're discussing here.

We're talking about getaways where you go for the sole purpose of refurbishing your spirit, regaining your inner strength. You go for quiet and contemplation.

Granted, you probably won't come back with a tan or a great deal on Native American beadwork, but you will come back with something better. Peace of mind. A brand-new way of looking at things.

The minute you walk through the gates of a spiritual community, you feel it. You're not sure what "it" is exactly, but you notice a rare sense of peace. You think to yourself, *Hmm, something's different here.*

Admittedly, spiritual retreats tend to be taken alone. You're going inward, after all. But a spiritual getaway can be even more meaningful when shared with like-minded seekers, which—what can I say?—is more likely to be your girlfriends than your main squeeze.

So whether you want to hear Trappist monks singing the liturgy, beat some drums yourself, or learn the principles of the Course in Miracles, stay tuned and I'll tell you about spiritual getaways with your girlfriends.

Amazing Place, How Sweet the Sound

Okay, you're ready for some time apart from the material world. You're ready for a spiritual getaway. First rule of thumb is you and your girlfriends will probably have to work a little harder to find the right location. Most travel agents have never heard of the Lama Foundation in San Cristobal, New Mexico, or Zen Mountain Monastery in Mount Tremper, New York. Nor will you find splashy ads to most convents in the travel section of the newspaper or the back of a magazine. In fact, it's quite likely your family and friends have never heard of a lot of these places either.

That's okay. Spiritual getaways are about stepping out of your normal comfort zone. They're about reaching for your best self, about learning and practicing your best values and taking them back to your regular life.

Like all the other girlfriend getaways, there are plenty of options when it comes to spiritual getaways.

For some, you needn't leave home. You can join an e-circle (as in *e-mail*) of like-minded women where every Monday or every other Wednesday you get together on the net to discuss the Course in Miracles or Zen Buddhism or whatever spiritual topic trips your trigger. These e-circles are pretty easy to find. Just type in "spiritual circle" on Google.com. The good thing about these "getaways" is that you and your best friend on the other side of the country do it together.

Or maybe there's a weekly spiritual getaway right outside your front door. In San Francisco, for example, girlfriends can partake of Red Tent gatherings. Maybe you've heard of the best-seller by Anita Diamonte about women from the Bible who were sent to a special exclusionary "red tent" during their menstrual periods. At these gatherings named for the book, girlfriends come together in a sacred circle to honor the stories of their lives and the lives of their mothers, aunts, and grandmothers. Each month for thirteen months, a different artist, performer, writer, or scholar leads the circle of girlfriends. But don't be fooled by the title. It's clearly a circle where everyone learns and everyone teaches. To find out more about the Red Tent gatherings, contact Alaura O'Dell at 888–779–6696.

What's the Difference Between an Abbey and a Monastery?

Abbey and *monastery* are practically synonymous. *Monastery* usually refers to the actual building where the monks live; an *abbey* is a monastery governed by an abbot. An *abbey* is typically self-supporting, and must have at least twelve monks (men or women) who have professed solemn vows and have an abbot as their religious superior. Five other terms that could come in handy:

1. **DIVINE OFFICE.** I know what you're thinking, but it's not a sacred desk and computer. The divine office is an official, formal liturgical prayer.
2. **MANTRA.** A sacred word or phrase that is repeated to quiet that derned Curious George, usually used in meditation.
3. **REFECTORY.** Monastery chow hall.
4. **POUSTINIA**. Translated it means the "silence of God." It's a designated period or place where a complete retreat, silence, fasting, and separation from normal activities take place.
5. **TAIZE.** A chant that was developed at a monastery in France that has spread through the world.

It's Not Just for Flying Nuns Anymore

Another option is to take a time-out at a monastery, abbey, or intentional community. Chances are there's one of these hermitages near you—a place where the nuns, priests, or some other variety of "spiritual gurus" offer simple rooms, simple meals, and a glimpse into their unique lifestyle. Monasteries and abbeys are located in every state in the country as well as overseas.

Most of these spiritual communities view your visit as a ministry of sorts. The good news is, they are not out to convert you. They offer rooms in a spirit of openness and warmth. In most cases there is no expectation that you'll attend their services or participate in meditations—but if you should choose to, you'll be welcomed with open arms.

Found on a Bed at a Monastery in Arizona

Dear Friend:

As I made this bed, I offered a prayer for whoever would sleep in it next. I prayed for your rest and a sense of peace; for the refreshment of your body and the renewal of your spirit.

I prayed that God would bless you with love, give you a sense of His presence, and comfort you with mercy and grace. I prayed [for] trust in God's love, which can bind us all together.

Some of these hermitages are Buddhist, others Christian or Jewish. Still others are Sufi while others are what some people call New Age. But never fear: Most accept and welcome people of all faiths.

Sometimes you'll be expected to pitch in with chores. You might have to bring your own linens or wash dishes after the meal. Such cheerful service, in many instances, is part of the spiritual practice.

There are also lots of tour companies that plan itineraries for spiritual seekers. Sacred Journeys for Women (888–779–6696 or www.sacredjourneys.com), for example, caters to girlfriends who resonate to ancient spiritual traditions, to what British-born founder Alaura O'Dell calls the "goddess energy." Designed exclusively for women, all Sacred Journeys pilgrimages include presentations on goddess mythology, transformational ceremonies, and intimate experiences of sacred sites using ceremony, informal lectures, healing circles, and dance. These women-only trips visit Hawaii, Ireland, England, Crete, and other places around the globe where women and "goddesses" have traditionally been honored.

What follows are nine spiritual retreats you can plan with your girlfriends.

1. Try a yoga camp. Wood Valley Temple and Retreat Center (808–928–8539 or www.nechung.org) on the island of Hawaii was dedicated by no less a spiritual force than the Dalai Lama himself. Not only do you enjoy the beauty of Hawaii, but you get to learn and practice yoga in a nonsectarian Tibetan Buddhist temple as well. Located south of the Hawaiian Volcanoes National Park, the retreat center is nested in a lush tropical valley between towering green mountains and shaded by giant eucalyptus trees.

Every morning and afternoon girlfriends can participate in sessions of Kripalu yoga, a gentle practice that harmonizes body, mind, and spirit. In the evening you learn breathing techniques. Each day at 7:00 A.M. and 7:00 P.M., the resident monk leads chanting in the temple. It's near the exotic Punalu-u Black Sand Beach, home of the rare hawksbill turtles, and the Hawaiian Volcanoes National Park, home of Pele, goddess of the Volcano.

Two vegetarian meals are served daily, with an abundance of organic vegetables and tropical fruits. Thai and Indian dinners are served from time to time. Programs run Thursday to Wednesday and can be booked for less than $1,000, depending on the type of accommodations you require.

2. *Really getting away in New Mexico.* You have to *really* want to get to the Monastery of Christ in the Desert: It's forty-five minutes from the nearest airport, 6,500 feet above sea level, and the closest phone is 15 miles away at Georgia O'Keeffe's Ghost Ranch. The 12-mile dirt road that leads to this gorgeous spot in Chaco Canyon is treacherous and often mired in mud. Even the local cows avoid it. It's not unusual for folks to abandon their vehicles altogether and walk in.

But once you're there, you just ring the porter's bell (at least eight times, so the monk who hosts guests can hear you) and you'll suddenly be transported to a quieter, more peaceful place in your heart. Just to make sure that you, as the guest host says, "get it," you can't stay for less than two days. It takes time to get away from life's hectic pace and fit into the monastic rhythm.

The monastery was founded by Father Aelred Well, a Benedictine priest who in 1964 came with two other monks from Pine City, New York. They enlisted George Nakashima, a famous woodworker, to design and build it. The three double rooms are perfect for you and a girlfriend or two. Since the key elements of Benedictine life are charity, prayer, spiritual reading, and manual labor, you'll be asked to chip in with chores. Meals—all vegetarian—are eaten in silence, although there may be a spiritual reading or music. You have to write ahead for reservations (as much as three months in advance in the summer), but the guestmaster does have an e-mail (guests@christ desert.org). The suggested donation is fifty dollars a night, but it is requested that people pay what they can. For more information, contact Monastery of Christ in the Desert, P.O. Box 270, Abiquiu, New Mexico 87510-0270, or www.christdesert.org.

3. Divine travels. If you and your girlfriends want to awaken your inner selves, consider an itinerary by Divine Travel (503-471-1608 or www.divinetravels.com). With trips to sacred sites in India, Bali, Egypt, Peru, Italy, and United States, Divine Travel was started by Susan Shumsky, a spiritual guru herself who was personally trained to teach yoga and meditation by Maharishi Mahesh Yogi, the same guy who worked with the Beatles.

For example, on the Sacred Bali trip, you not only experience the culture of Bali and visit famous mask makers, but you participate in private ceremonies at ancient temples and healing springs.

Shumsky, who leads the tours, is also a successful jewelry designer as well as the author of *Divine Revelation,* a best-selling book about accessing your spiritual power. In January 2001 she led a tour of thirty people to the Maha Kumb Mela, a spiritual festival on the banks of the Ganges that occurs only once every 144 years. More than a hundred million people attended, including the Dalai Lama, Madonna, and Paul McCartney.

4. Transformation at Pendle Hill. Founded by Quakers in 1930, Pendle Hill (800-742-3150 or www.pendlehill.org) is a twenty-three-acre retreat center that offers weeklong courses in everything from cooking the Quaker way to writing personal memoirs to experimenting with light. You and your girlfriends can even take a course in understanding Shakespeare.

Quakers at Pendle Hill have four basic philosophies, and even if you're not a Quaker, these transformational beliefs can come in handy. They are: (1) equality and respect for everyone, (2) simplicity, (3) harmony of inward and outward actions, and (4) community as a powerful tool for seeking Spirit.

Besides the weeklong courses, you can also come for what they call "Sojourns." Pendle Hill offers two rustic hermitages—the Spring House, a small cabin nestled in a bamboo grove, and Flower House, a spacious room near the campus. On a sojourn, you're free to use the library and art studios, share meals, and attend daily worship. If you and two girlfriends can come up with a peace and social justice project, you can even apply for the Frances R. Dewing and Geraldine Burd Scholarship which will give you a room for free.

5. Counting to Zen and back. Want to know what a monk does? At Zen Mountain Monastery (845–688–2228 or www.mro.org) you and your girlfriends can take monastic training in Zen Buddhism. Set on 230 gorgeous acres in the Catskill Mountains of upstate New York, this center offers introductory weekends and weeklong silent meditation retreats (known as sesshin), as well as retreats in martial arts, Buddhist studies, and other subjects that American Zen monks might benefit from.

The ancient spiritual tradition of Zen Buddhism dates back 2,500 years and uses zazen, a type of meditation, to guide you deep within yourself to uncover inherent wisdom and compassion. It's not an easy thing to learn.

Your day here starts at 5:00 A.M. (except during the spring and fall, when it changes to 4:30 A.M.), lights are out at 9:00 P.M. The accommodation are dorms, the meals are primarily vegetarian and you're not allowed to bring your own food. Why would you go? Enlightenment with a big *E*.

6. Rooms with a view. On a clear day—and everyone knows it never rains in southern California—at Mount Calvary Monastery (805–962–9855 or www.mount-calvary.org), you can see 40 miles to Point Magoo and 25

Curious George
or Meditation and Why It's Next to Impossible to Quiet the Mind

If you've ever tried to meditate, you've probably made the acquaintance of Curious George, the crazy monkey mind who begins chattering every time you begin to meditate. George, of course, is particularly curious to know, *Is she doing this right?* He also wonders what you're going to have for dinner, why your husband refused to put down the lid to the toilet seat this morning, and whether or not you're going to hear from your boss about that promotion. Monkey mind, as astute meditators call it, is the voice that goes everywhere except for "into the stillness."

According to meditators in the know, the trick is to thank the voice for sharing and then let it go. Return to the breathing or the mantra or whatever tool you're using to train your mind. Over and over again, just bring your mind back to your meditation practice. Eventually, Curious George will get curious about something or somebody else. That's not to say he won't return. After all, even serious meditators sometimes wonder, *Is this a waste of time? Can I really afford those shoes?* and *I think I'll have a pastrami sandwich for lunch.*

---

miles to the Channel Islands. Let's just say the views of the Pacific coastline would make a believer out of the brittlest of defectors.

The Episcopalian monks are happy to share this gorgeous lookout perched 1,250 feet above Santa Barbara. In the large Spanish-style house are thirty guest rooms, tastefully decorated with religious art. There's also a tasty buffet in the refectory, mountain hiking in Rattlesnake Canyon—a nature preserve that reaches 20 miles—a library, and a bookstore. The monastery was established in 1947 by Father Karl Tiedemann and the monks are there to pray, both as an act of praise to God and as an intercession for the needs of the world.

7. *Sister act*. Located in the quiet town of Mount Angel, Oregon, the Shalom Prayer Center (503–845–6773 or www.open.org/~shalom), a ministry of Queen of Angels Monastery of Benedictine sisters, has been around since 1882. Not only can you take all kinds of workshops and classes—ranging from "using poetry to zest up your inner life" to "aging gracefully" to "using the Jungian anagram"—but you can also garden side by side with the forty-plus sisters who call this monastery home.

The monastery orchard has apple, pear, plum, cherry, and quince trees as well as a grape arbor. Close by are the foothills of the Cascade Mountains and the beauty of Mount Hood. You'll eat from the fifteen acres of flower and vegetable gardens and be invited to join the sisters in prayer each day at 8:00 A.M. and 5:00 P.M. at the Shalom Chapel and at the monastery on Sunday.

There are several vineyards in the area, which is probably best known for its Oktoberfest, a four-day celebration when some 350,000 show up to party.

8. *Fifth wheel in a fifth world*. Fifth World Pilgrimages (619–595–0215 or www.fifthworld.com) were started by Charlene Selsvold, a Jungian psychotherapist who specializes in the study of mythology. Her spiritual getaways focus on the transformative power of mythic imagination. She proudly calls her trips pilgrimages and thinks each should be a potent tool for learning about the world and yourself.

Each year she leads a "Journey of the Feminine Spirit Retreat" in Mexico where girlfriends do sunrise yoga, take mystical walks on the white sands of the Yucatan Peninsula, and reactivate what she calls the "Goddess self." She also offers several trips to Bhutan.

9. *The hills are alive*. The Abbey of St. Walburga (970–484–1887 or www.walburga.org) was started in 1935 by three girlfriends (well, actually they were Benedictine nuns) who had fled from Europe and Nazi persecution. They landed on 150 acres just outside Boulder, Colorado, that the first Catholic bishop of Denver had purchased way back in 1867. Since nothing had been done with the beautiful property, the sisters had their work cut out for them. They repaired the leaky house, propped up the dilapidated barn, and managed to eke out a meager existence thanks to helpful neighbors who loaned them farm equipment. They stayed in Boulder until they grew out of that location and moved to the Virginia Dale area, roughly halfway between Fort Collins and Laramie, Wyoming.

Their main purpose is the divine office, which means they gather seven times a day to sing and pray. Using adaptations of Gregorian chants (the abbess spent four years translating liturgy and compiling books so visitors can sing along), their prayer is music to anyone's ear. In between these seven canonical hours, they manage to raise cattle, sheep, and llamas, tend a garden, bake bread, embroider vestments, and weave llama wool.

At the retreat house that's about three-quarters of a mile from the main abbey, girlfriends can bunk in the simple lodging and take part in abbey-sponsored retreats or individual retreats.

True-Life Tale
Wild Liberation

THE GIRLFRIENDS:
1. Vanessa, thirty-six, who works in marketing and business development in Atlanta.
2. The new friends Vanessa met on her retreat.

THE MISSION:
To let her hair down through belly dancing, mask making, drumming, meditating, and sharing.

THE DESTINATION:
"A Weekend for Wild Women" at Coolfont Resort (800–888–8768 or www.coolfont.com) in Berkeley Springs, West Virginia. Known as the Wild Woman Capital of the World, this town has three times as many massage therapists as lawyers, five spas, and even a Wild Woman Shop that sells Wild Woman salsa. Recently voted one of the top twelve art destinations in America, many of its premier businesses are owned by women, including Tari's Café—which offers an all-girl, all-day jam session called Torch and Twang.

THE GETAWAY *(as told by Vanessa):*
"Last spring I decided it was time to take a vacation and go someplace that I'd never been before. My original plan was to get together with a couple of girlfriends and go off somewhere for a nice long weekend. However, to my great disappointment, our timing was completely off. Then I pondered the unthinkable—for

me—to take a trip alone. I had never done anything like that before. It was exciting, yet at the same time very scary; but I had no choice—I *needed* to get away!

"I searched the Internet for places of interest. Money was definitely an object, so my options seemed very limited. Then I happened across a link that took me to the Web page for Berkeley Springs. Hallelujah! The write-up about the 'Wild Women Weekend' appealed as an opportunity to do something daring in the company of other forward-thinking women, relatively inexpensively. Having recently been divorced and suffering through serious financial hardship, I felt I was losing my zest for living. I had to get back my confidence—or better yet take what little I had left and rebuild it.

"When I arrived, Kim, our Group Leader, asked each of us to share a brief bio about ourselves and why we chose to be a part of the gathering. It was interesting to hear the events in each woman's life that led her there. I listened intently and realized that some of their stories seemed so very familiar. By evening's end, I was well on my way to making new friends.

"The time spent with the 'Wild Women' of the group felt like the beginnings of forming a sisterhood. We shared our experiences—some painful, some joyful—and I learned how to release myself and allow my guard to drop, at least for the time being.

"For me the high point of the weekend involved a primal celebration of womanhood through drumming and dancing. Everyone who participated was given the opportunity to choose a costume, making the occasion a lot more festive. A bright-colored cloth caught my eye. I also wore a makeshift headpiece and beads, which gave me the look of a native princess. I was ready to dance!

"I was truly in my element, my spirit buoyed by the rhythms of the drums. This was wonderful therapy for my soul. I felt empowered. My womanhood was affirmed by the experience and that night will forever be etched in my memory.

"In fact, the entire weekend was far more enriching than I could have ever imagined. I was free to be vulnerable around others, and came away feeling totally recharged and revitalized."

—*Thanks to Vanessa Headley for providing this True-Life Tale.*

Shopping Getaways

Why God Created Credit Cards

> "WHEN WOMEN GET DEPRESSED, THEY GO SHOPPING. WHEN MEN GET DEPRESSED, THEY INVADE OTHER COUNTRIES."
>
> —Elayne Boosler, comedian

This is the chapter where we finally come out of the closet. Where we willingly give up the pretense and the false claims we might have made about traveling because we wanted to see this museum or because we wanted to visit that national landmark.

In this chapter we girlfriends are finally going to admit that the main reason we adore girlfriend getaways is . . . are you really ready to come clean, sisters? . . . because we can shop without significant male others looking over our shoulders. We plan these getaways because we long to find bargains "there" that we'd never find "here."

TALKING: ★★★

Just remember: There's no such thing as a quiet shopping mall. You'll be gasping, panting, and uttering such phrases as "Ohmigosh, you're never going to believe this!" as you make your way around the mall or down Fifth Avenue. You'll have ample conversational (not to mention gloating) opportunities when you proudly lay out your new purchases on the bed (and desk and bathroom sink) in your hotel room.

 **GAWKING:** ★★★★

It depends on what you want to gawk at. I don't need to tell you that men, typically, are not known for their shopping savvy. But what could be more appealing to the eye than little signs that read 50 PERCENT OFF or BUY ONE, GET ONE FREE?

 **ROCKING:** ★★★★

If you're wise enough to avoid heels on your daytime shopping excursions, you'll likely have plenty of energy left for nighttime rocking. After all, you've got to go somewhere to show off that new Coach handbag.

 DOCKING: ★★★★

The world's best shopping is always near the world's best lodging (they're practically synonymous these days now that most resorts offer on-site boutiques and arcades), so rest assured, the hotel bed on which you lay your purchases will be swanky. As will the rest of the hotel. Besides, you get to live a lifestyle you probably don't enjoy at home.

I mean, sure, the Arc de Triomphe is nice to have in the background of a photograph, but why we really want to go to Paris, what we truly want to see is Prisunic, Charles Jourdan, and other shops on Champs-Élysées. The Statue of Liberty might make a great key chain (any traveler worth her kitschy souvenir collection simply must have one), but why we really love New York can be summed up in three (or four) words: Bloomingdale's, Barneys, and Bergdorf Goodman.

It's probably best not to admit this little secret to the significant others in your life—particularly if they have any kind of vested interest in your credit card balance. But as my old friend Beatrice used to say, "God wouldn't have invented plastic if he didn't want his sons (and daughters) to shop."

And look at it this way: A true shopping getaway provides many important benefits.

1. Exercise. It takes a good set of lungs to walk up and down both sides of Fifth Avenue. And when was the last time you clocked the distance from one end of the Mall of America to the other? Shopping all day requires incredible stamina. It combines that all-important Jane Fonda–touting aerobic exercise with the anaerobic sport of weight lifting. Those shopping bags, after all, can get heavy.

2. Education. What can I say? Seeing Fendi skirts in person and trying on spindly-heeled Manolo Blahnik pumps should be required girlfriend learning. Whoever told you that seeing them on *Sex and the City* is enough?

3. Economics lessons. It's a well-known fact that from seventh grade on, girls lose ground when it comes to math problems. That's only because their mothers didn't encourage them early on to compare prices on Prada handbags.

Clothes Encounters

> **"REMEMBER WE NEED EACH OTHER. WHEN OUR PANTIES ARE DOWN AND THERE'S NO MORE TOILET PAPER IN THE LADIES ROOM, IT'S THE WOMAN IN THE NEXT STALL WE'RE ALWAYS GOING TO TURN TO FOR HELP."**
>
> —Susan Jane Gilman, *Kiss My Tiara: How to Rule the World as a Smartmouth Goddess*

A shopping getaway with the girlfriends requires the planning of a small-scale military invasion. You don't, after all, want to just wander around casually, snatching up anything that catches your eye. You have to be vigilant, know what you really need, and to know that you have the means to buy.

What follows are tips and insider secrets for planning your next shopping getaway:

1. Be prepared. Before you so much as set one foot on an airplane, you and your girlfriends should read up on your destination of choice. That's what guidebooks and the Internet are for. Divide the research up. Cindy, you research Via Montenapoleone (it's a street in Milan, in case you're wondering); Lou, you take Corso Venezia. Find out what stores are there and what they're known for. Find out when the big sales take place. Be well versed on what's really a bargain in which place. Furs and shoes, for example, are   good buys in Toronto. Real vanilla is sold for a song in Mexico. If you're looking for factory outlets, New England is the place to go. The Midwest has great bargains on antiques.

2. Take an organized shopping tour. If you and your girlfriends just don't have the heart for all that planning and you're all bad at directions (maybe the last time you went looking for that boutique written up in *Vanity Fair*, you ended up in Teabucket, Ohio), you may want to consider an organized shopping tour. Thousands of companies offer tours of the world's great shopping meccas. Fashion Update, for example, takes groups to all the best haunts in New York most Fridays between 10:00 A.M. and 5:00 P.M. Rates range from $175 per person (up to three hours for a group of about ten) to $300 per person (three hours for two people). Private tours and hourly rates can also be negotiated (888–447–2846 or www.fashionupdate.com).

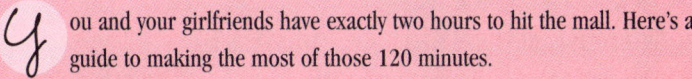

Guerrilla Guide to Navigating a Shopping Mall

You and your girlfriends have exactly two hours to hit the mall. Here's a guide to making the most of those 120 minutes.

1. *Wear sneakers.*

2. *Avoid parking near the doors of the big anchor department stores.* Yes, you may have to walk a bit farther (that's what the sneakers are for), but you'll save big chunks of time by not having to circle the parking lot a dozen times.

3. *Pee at the nearest men's store.* I know you normally don't hang out at men's stores (unless, of course, you're buying a birthday gift for your dad), but it's a little-known secret that men's stores also have women's rest rooms, and they're usually the cleanest and least crowded in the mall.

4. *Dining? Don't mess with it.* You can usually find better food outside the mall.

5. *Add a few minutes to your shopping trip* by crossing other time-consuming items off your to-do list. Lots of malls offer nontraditional services such as film developing, banking, and nail polishing.

Ten Best Places to Drop a Cool Million

1. **DUBAI.** Okay, so you'll probably have to keep your knees covered, but in the souks of this Arab country you can score incredible bargains on spices, exotic perfumes, and electronics. Even the airport has incredible prices on just about anything your heart could desire. Dubai International Airport has even been known to host car raffles (if you win, they'll ship your prize home for free) and million-dollar giveaways.

2. **CHAMPS-ÉLYSÉES AND AVENUE MONTAIGNE, PARIS.** Let's just say the art of the window display was invented here (at Hermes in 1922), so even if you don't want to drop a million, you can window-shop until your mouth drops. If you want to visit the top couture houses and rub elbows with such designers as Chanel, Christian Dior, and Prada, stick with Avenue Montaigne. If you're more interested in the Gap and the Disney Store (of course, why go to Paris for that?), check out Champs-Élysées—which, according to many globe-trotters, is the most beautiful avenue in the world.

3. **RODEO DRIVE, BEVERLY HILLS, CALIFORNIA.** It may be only three blocks long, but boy, can you do some damage to your wallet in those three short blocks. It's where kids' shoes can cost $400 and to get in the door you practically have to show your family tree. The newest and most pretentious addition is Two Rodeo, a strip of boutiques complete with fountains and Italian piazza.

4. **MILAN, ITALY.** What you see in Milan will be in style in America (and everywhere else) in a year. Can you say *good taste?* Can you say *fashion savvy?* This is where international garmentos go to find the goods they tote back to Hong Kong to reproduce as inexpensive copies. Elegant boutiques and posh cafes are found in charming Victorian-era buildings. Be sure to check out La Rinascente, Milan's own department store, and Provers, a must for vintage wine selection.

5. **BAHNHOFSTRASSES, ZURICH, SWITZERLAND.** Swiss watches aren't the only things you'll find at the more than 120 shops on this pristine street. No dealing with honking cars, because all 1.4 kilometers of tree-lined streets are closed to everything but foot traffic and trams.

6. BOND STREET, LONDON, ENGLAND. Bond, Street Bond, located in the exclusive Mayfair District, has been a favorite of the rich and famous since the 1850s. Name a famous designer (Armani? Versace? Cartier?) and you'll find his or her work showcased in former homes of England's most famous politicians, artists, and writers. Phillips and Sotheby's auction houses make for a free and fun break.

7. FIFTH AVENUE, MANHATTAN. Of course, there's Saks, Bloomingdales, Macy's, and other upscale department stores, but you'll also find designer shops such as Gucci, Tiffany, and Versace. A good time to go is around the Christmas holidays, when doormen dress up as toy soldiers (at FAO Schwarz) and Saks puts on its holiday window show.

8. THE MAGNIFICENT MILE, CHICAGO. It's just a few blocks off Lake Michigan, but Chicago's Michigan Avenue has all the department store greats plus lots of locals such as Bigsby, Kruthers, and Crate & Barrel.

9. AVINGUDA DIAGONAL, BARCELONA, SPAIN. All the top designers are found here, along with wonderful outdoor cafes and art galleries.

10. THE GINZA DISTRICT, TOKYO, JAPAN. It's only eight Tokyo blocks, but it has some of the most expensive real estate on earth. The fourteen-story Marion has seven movie theaters and two department stores. Check out the clock on Tokyo's most famous department store, Mitsukoshi, Wako.

3. Take ample luggage. Slip a foldable bag into your luggage to use as a carry-on for the trip home.

4. Strike while the iron is hot. If something you like is ridiculously cheap, go ahead and buy in bulk. Stick your purchases in a gift drawer at home and get them out for housewarmings or birthday parties.

5. Think basic. Speaking of gifts, simple things like a tube of Crest labeled in Hebrew make great gifts. My daughter's foreign toothpaste collection includes samples from New Zealand, Korea, Paris, and Mexico. A stop at a chemist (in England) or a pharmacie (in France) will yield all sorts of moderately priced body-care products that will become novelties at home. Wrap the gifts in cartoon pages from foreign newspapers, and don't forget to buy foreign gift cards as well.

6. *Avoid state sales tax.* This one can get tricky, particularly if you're eager to show off your new purchases at a nightclub that evening. But keep in mind that the patrons of the nightclub have never seen your old clothes, and that by shipping your purchases home, you can ask to be excused from paying state sales tax. Granted, postage ain't cheap, but if you're buying expensive lightweight scarves (for example), you can save a bundle. Oh, and while you're giving them your address, ask to be on their mailing list.

7. *Get a museum membership.* You know those museums that most big cities have? They all have gift shops, really cool gift shops with really cool gifts. If one of you buys a membership to the museum (usually somewhere in the neighborhood of $25), all of you can get a discount (anywhere from 10 to 25 percent) in the museum shop.

8. *Shop the exchange rates*. Yes, this takes some financial savvy, but if you keep up on the exchange rates between the American dollar and the currency of your country of choice, you can plan your trip for when the exchange rate is in your favor. The American dollar can go a long way against a Mexican peso. Even in Canada, a women-only cross-country ski package at Whistler's Pan Pacific Lodge (888–905–9995) that includes two nights in a two-bedroom suite, ski lessons, a fondue dinner for four, and a tote bag with PowerBars, fudge, salmon jerky, and springwater was advertised recently for $2,210 in Canadian dollars—only $1,425 in U.S. dollars at the time.

9. *Buyer beware*—or, everything you need to know about street shopping. I'm actually a big fan of those fast-talking hucksters on the streets. But then, I like fake designer watches and copies of Versace handbags. I even bought a videotape once of *Bram Stoker's Dracula* that hadn't even hit the video stores yet. My clever salesman had taken a video camera to the theaters and made his own pirate copy. Illegal, I know, but it was fun to show the folks at home.

10. Take advantage of department stores. Thanks to all the competition out there from discount stores, factory outlets, and good old Wal-Mart, the venerable old department stores have had to devise new strategies just to retain a decent market share. That's good news for you and your girlfriends. Many of the tony department stores now have personal shoppers, restaurants, exercise studios, makeup artists, translators, and shipping services. Plus, they have big sales. Like everybody else, they have to unload merchandise, too.

11. Know your factory outlets. You probably won't have to go far if you just want to make a day of factory outlet shopping. Malls with "factory outlet stores" have sprung up everywhere. Keep in mind that there are real factory outlets (actually located in factories, such as the Reebok outlet store in Stoughton, Massachusetts), fake factory outlets, manufacturers' factory outlets (the Dooney & Bourke in Norwalk, Connecticut, has a great once-a-year sale), and jobbers who buy from many sources and sell at discounted prices. For a comprehensive list of factory outlets around the country, contact Outlet Bound, Box 1255, Orange, CT 06477 (800–336–8853 or www.outletbound.com).

12. Have tea. After you've been shopping all day, you're going to need to get off your feet for a while. Many fancy hotels (you can go even if you're staying at Day's Inn) host afternoon teas, often in the English tradition with scones and jam and tea sandwiches.

True-Life Tale
Chicago Minus Men

THE GIRLFRIENDS:
1. Jayne, lifestyle editor, *Mpls.St.Paul Magazine.*
2. Dawn, a docent in Chicago.
3. Shelly, a publishing sales rep in the Twin Cities.
4. Trish, owner of a promotional company, also in the Twin Cities.

THE MISSION:
To shop until they dropped.

THE DESTINATION:
Chicago's famed Michigan Avenue.

THE GETAWAY *(as told by Jayne)*:
"Nearly every travel experience involves some type of shopping—whether you buy from Chiang Mai's night markets, the street vendors on New York's Canal Street, or peddlers pounding the sands in Mexico. But sometimes I travel for the sole purpose of shopping. And for those of us in flyover territory, a jaunt to Chicago is the easiest way to get our ya-yas.

"This story begins fifteen years ago on my maiden voyage to Chicago (all trips since have been defined by it), when my twenty-something roommates and I took a road trip there to celebrate the New Year. I went for the nightlife, but fell in love with the shopping. Back in 1986 Chicago offered much that I couldn't find here: Saks Fifth Avenue, Neiman Marcus, I. Magnin, Tiffany, Lord & Taylor, Bonwit Teller, Crate & Barrel, and, of course, Marshall Field's. Never had I seen such delights. I purchased a hat at Saks, packaged in a black lacquer hatbox with a red-rope handle. I was never the same.

"That was then. Now Minneapolis has Saks, Neiman, C & B—and, of course, Field's. Bonwit and I. Magnin are history; Lord & Taylor has moved downmarket. And why leave home when you've got the biggest mall in America? I'll tell you why: Because no matter how you slice it, this ain't Chicago, where shopping is an experience to be savored.

"Nothing against husbands, but shopping with your man is like a no-fat latte. Who else but the girls will spend an entire afternoon at Lori's Designer Shoes, hang out for an hour at the Barneys cosmetic counter, or have the patience to shop ten stores for "just the right handbag"?

"So in March, Shelly, Trish, and I spent three days and nights on and off Michigan Avenue. I was Margaret Mead, studying the habits of the natives and making sure we didn't miss anything.

"Our plan was to shop till we, well, dropped. But once we checked into our swank junior suite at The Peninsula Hotel, plans unraveled. Then open just under a year, we could already tell The Pen would undoubtedly lock horns with the nearby Ritz-Carlton for Zagat's Best U.S. City Hotel honors. We loved our room overlooking the historic Water Tower. (Double sinks, tasteful furnishings, surround-sound audio—although, while primping for dinner, we were paid a visit by security and asked to turn down Nelly Furtado. Oops.) From our roost, we could view the hustle-bustle of the shoppers below—like little ants—calling us to hit the pavement and join them. But the whirlpools, lap pools, gym, spa, and yoga room (all on the nineteenth and twentieth floors, surrounded by walls of floor-to-ceiling windows) called louder. A trip to the steam room became part of our morning regimen.

"Most of our time was spent within a mile of The Peninsula. Within this zone is the best shopping Chicago has to offer, from the big-name department stores to the small boutiques. Dawn, a Chicago pal who joined us for most of the trip, says her New York friends are envious of Chicago because everything is so close by. Who isn't? Our three days were built around sushi, martinis, shoes, champagne, and shopping—not necessarily in that order. The first two defined our evenings, the latter three directed our days. It was like a *Sex and the City* episode without the sex.

"On Friday we headed north to boutiqueville, anchored by Oak Street, a three-block stretch of style and couture where Michigan Avenue abuts the lake. The fashionista haunts include the very tony designer shops of Nicole Miller, Betsey Johnson, Jil Sander, St. John, Hermes, and Kate Spade, plus Ultimo and Ikram, which offer a mix of designers. While in the 'hood, we stopped at CRU—a glamour-puss wine bar and cafe. We loved the sweet potato soup and BLT-style beef tenderloin sandwiches so much we hit the place two days in a row. (Or maybe it was the champagne flights and the twenty crystal chandeliers.) On nearby blocks we shopped Barneys New York, Anthropologie, Urban Outfitters, Prada, Diesel, BCBG, Sur La Table (Ampersand meets Kitchen Window), and modern home furnishings stores Portico and Ligne Roset. Another favorite was Material Possessions for home accessories.

"Saturday, on the advice of the locals, we navigated Armitage Avenue two miles north—specifically to shop Lori's Designer Shoes, a compact, boutique-style DSW. No need to cut through the clutter to get to the good stuff. We loved the shoes, the help-yourself service, and the prices. It was obvious we were sharing the mirrors with locals. You can't leave this place with fewer than two pairs of shoes and a handbag. The challenge is to keep it to that. Limit your Armitage explorations to the blocks between Halsted and Sheffield and visit Lori's, Cynthia Rowley, Art Effect, Isis, JB & Me, and Soapstone—just a few of our picks. Before wrapping it up for the day, we paid homage to Rachel Ashwell at her Shabby Chic boutique, just a block from the hotel.

"We saved Michigan Avenue for Sunday. At times we split up (bring the cell phone)—the four-story Banana Republic for me, FAO Schwarz for the moms—but we agreed on a champagne rendezvous at the Ralph Lauren Café. Three glasses of Tattinger and $36 later, we were off. We skipped American Girl, next door to Lauren, but it's a favorite pilgrimage for moms and daughters.

(During our whirlpool soaks, we spied little girls swimming while their American Girl dolls lounged on poolside chaises.)

"Working our way south on Michigan, we hit Chicago Place (including its gorgeous Saks and Room & Board), plus the nearby Tiffany, mega Crate & Barrel, and Kenneth Cole as we made our way to the Shops at North Bridge (the new mall—and a beauty). Highlights were Nordstrom (more shoes) and Vosges Haut-Chocolat (chocolates mixed with exotic spices—think *Chocolat,* the movie). Our northbound trip on the east side of the street included Niketown, Sony, and Neiman Marcus. Water Tower Place (and its Marshall Field's) had to wait until next time. (I actually prefer the State Street Field's with its fabulous period interiors, the famous clocks, and Tiffany dome.)

"Our weekend was a whirlwind of laughing, crying, gossiping, and people-watching. (I get the whole Burberry plaid thing now. It was everywhere! Including adorning a coat on a black pug we met in the hotel elevator.) Last words? Bring your hippest clothes, including your most fashion-forward shoes and handbags. To shop Chicago in style—you need to be in style. As Dawn reminded us, you can spot suburbanites by their shoes."

—*Thanks to Jayne Haugen Olson for providing this True-Life Tale.*

Now That You're Broke

*n*ow that you've spent your million, you may be forced to be on the lookout for bargains. Since shopping has never been easier on the Net, check out www.Members.tripod.com/atouchoffreebies for lots of free things. You can get everything from free Ray-Bans to free pet treats on your cat's birthday to diapers for your new baby.

World's Thirty-two Best Chick Flicks

"Women make the best psychoanalysts—until they fall in love. After that, they make the best patients."

—Psychoanalyst to Ingrid Bergman in the movie *Spellbound*

Movies, as you undoubtedly know, are much more than mindless entertainment. Find the right film, administer it with something high in fat grams, and your problems are practically solved. Although they're sometimes difficult to spot at the video store (being as how they're often wedged between *Terminator* and *Rambo XVX*), here is *The Girlfriend Getaway Guide* list of the world's best chick flicks:

1. *The Joy Luck Club*
2. *Steel Magnolias*
3. *Enchanted April*
4. *Romy and Michelle's High School Reunion*
5. *Mystic Pizza*
6. *Desperately Seeking Susan*
7. *A League of Their Own*
8. *The Turning Point*
9. *When Denise Calls Up*
10. *Legally Blonde*
11. *A Little Princess*
12. *Nine to Five*
13. *Norma Rae*
14. *Coal Miner's Daughter*
15. *Muriel's Wedding*
16. *Gorillas in the Mist*
17. *Marvin's Room*
18. *Fried Green Tomatoes*
19. *Julia*
20. *Thelma and Louise*
21. *The Color Purple*
22. *Boys on the Side*
23. *Soul Food*
24. *Waiting to Exhale*
25. *Hannah and Her Sisters*
26. *Strangers in Good Company*
27. *The Women*
28. *Beaches*
29. *Circle of Friends*
30. *Foxfire*
31. *Now and Then*
32. *Divine Secrets of the Ya-Ya Sisterhood*

True-Life Tale

Egan, Minnesota, Here We Come!

THE GIRLFRIENDS:
1. Roberta, former VP of corporate services for the largest health-care network in Wisconsin.
2. Jeri, a psychologist in Milwaukee.
3. Neena, also a Milwaukee psychologist.
4. Esther, finance professor at the University of Wisconsin.

THE MISSION:
To enjoy winnings from "Cher Girlfriend Getaway" contest sponsored by the Egan, Minnesota, Visitors Bureau.

THE DESTINATION:
Egan, Minnesota, with a complimentary side trip to the Mall of America, the world's largest mall.

THE GETAWAY:
In September Roberta saw an ad in the *Milwaukee Journal* about an essay contest to win a weekend trip to Egan, Minnesota, to see Cher in concert. She and her girlfriends, during their regular Monday-evening game of mah-jongg, began taking turns writing the required fifty-five-word essay. The finishing touches were put on by Roberta, who, her girlfriends say, is a "poet laureate."

Normally six girlfriends play "mahj" on Mondays, and since only four can play mah-jongg at a time, the other two worked on the essay contest. Finally after discussing the week's events, the essay, and their mahj game, Roberta thought their poem was good enough and told everyone to "save the date, we're going to win!"

Sure enough, their essay (see the sidebar) was the winner out of nearly 400 entries that included everything from touching tributes to rap songs.

Says Roberta: "We had so much fun. Every time any of us talks about it we start giggling. We felt like a bunch of high school kids playing hooky! We drove five and a half hours from Milwaukee. We documented every event with photos . . . including our lunch stop at Wendy's and the 2:00 A.M. emergency visit by the hotel maintenance man when the bathroom tub-shower handle broke and we couldn't turn the water off (we were all in our flannel PJs and couldn't stop laughing).

"The concert was great. Cyndi Lauper was the opening act. When she sang 'Girls Just Wanna Have Fun' we all whipped out our cell phones and called home so our hubbies . . . or our answering machines . . . could share in the ambience of the evening.

"We had a great time at the Mall of America . . . rode the roller coaster, had a lovely lunch, shopped. The most special thing is we decided to go to Glamour Shots. We couldn't talk one of the girls into doing it but three of us had our makeup and hair done and dressed up in slinky stuff and posed for pictures, which we bought as gifts for our husbands. This was so much fun! Again . . . we felt like teenagers!

"Both evenings we stayed up until all hours playing mahj and eating popcorn and chocolates, drinking a little wine, and generally feeling relaxed and under no family or work demands.

"We all like Cher but none of us are what you would call fans. We would have enjoyed this as much had it been any big-name entertainer. The concert was wonderful . . . very nostalgic as we are just about the same age as Cher (55, 54, 54, and 50) and we all grew up with her . . . through the 1960s, 1970s, and beyond. Most of us still have our original bodies, however, and that's a constant area of growth."

The Award-Winning Essay:
Why We Deserve to "Cher" a Girlfriend Getaway

Age, sage, wear and tear,

Lots of flare.

Boobs sag, tush drags, eyes have bags.

Hormones crash

Hot Flash, Gotta dash.

Kids gone, swan song?

Wrinkle free we gotta be.

Done it all.

Stand tall!

Youth is fleeting.

Can't stop eating.

Memory gone, but going strong.

Men no longer stare.

Girlfriends Share.

WE NEED THIS!

Luxury Getaways

Life on the Trail of Julia Roberts

"I FEEL THERE IS SOMETHING UNEXPLORED ABOUT WOMEN THAT ONLY A WOMAN CAN EXPLORE."

—Georgia O'Keeffe, *artist*

Every now and then you gotta splurge. You have to say to yourself, *You know, there is more to life than money and I don't really care what this costs. I deserve the best and I'm going to go for it.*

So there!

Yes, this is the expensive chapter. The chapter where I discuss those once-in-a-lifetime getaways with your girlfriends, the kind of getaways Robin Leach would give his eyeteeth to film if he should happen to get wind of it. Course, I'm not going to tell.

 **TALKING:** ★★★★

More like moaning. Chances are your mouth will drop open and won't close until you hit the hotel's Beautyrest that night. The phrase you're bound to use repeatedly goes something like this: *I can't believe this!* or *Ohmigod, wait until I tell the folks back home!* Or (and this is combined with an elbow in the ribs to the girlfriend in nearest proximity) *Cindy, Cindy, look over there, isn't that Leo DiCaprio or Lucy Liu or ____?* Not only will a luxury getaway give you plenty of talking opportunities, but you'll probably still be talking about it for years to come.

 GAWKING: ★★★★

Move over Grand Canyon. The scenery at a luxury getaway is guaranteed to be hunkalicious.

 **ROCKING:** ★★★★

Think *Hard Rock Café*, think *Sex and the City*, think dancing the night away.

 **DOCKING:** ★★★★

Some of those *Can you believe this?* remarks will probably be uttered about your room. Suffice it to say luxurious lodging is unparalleled.

Maybe you and your girlfriends will want to charter a yacht or visit the hotel where *Pretty Woman* was filmed. Or indulge in the "Cartier Package" from Vancouver's Metropolitan Hotel, which includes a limo ride to Cartier, sterling-silver gifts, and champagne and chocolate-covered strawberries left in your room.

The book opened with getaways in your hometown. The way I see it, it might as well go out with a bang.

But I Live in Muncie, Indiana

Okay, so you and your girlfriends need a little help planning a luxurious, one-of-a-kind getaway. Believe me, they're not hard to find. If you read *People* magazine, *Town and Country*, *InStyle,* or any of the thousands of other celebrity rags out there, you'll find all sorts of ideas. Or check out *Robb Report*, which bills itself as the magazine "For the Luxury Lifestyle."

If that fails, try any of the following one-of-a-kind getaways.

1. Charter Your Own Yacht. You and your girlfriends have two choices. You can either take a cruise with 2,000 strangers—or you can charter your own cruise. Granted, your own yacht won't provide team beer chugging, Mexican combos playing "Feelings" on mariachis, or tour directors who, during the scheduled two-hour "shore adventure," steer you in and out of seashell museums.

In fact, should you and your girlfriends opt to charter a yacht, you're going to be called upon to make a lot of your own decisions. Like in which sun-drenched paradise should your yacht-for-the-week meet you? Do you prefer hopping among pristine uninhabited beaches or do you relish hours-long stretches of fast, open sea sailing?

Charter yachts provide the same basic amenities as a cruise ship: luxurious, private cabins, a skipper to work the sails, a choice of water toys (everything from fishing poles to Jet Skis), and a haute cuisine menu. Or if you'd rather, you can sleep on the deck, man your own sails, throw the toys overboard, and eat at island restaurants. The point is, it's up to you: where you dock, when you eat, what you wear or don't wear.

What's more, your own yacht can be had for as little as $1,000 per person per week. The average price for a commercial cruise is $1,300. The 1,500 or so crewed yachts available for charter range from 30 to 200-plus feet. The great majority fall in the 30- to 50-foot range and can accommodate four to six girlfriends, as well as a crew of two or three.

And while you won't get the cruise liners' stomach-bloating eight meals a day, you will get three meals prepared by such first mates as Penny Cadogan, a Cordon Bleu chef who has cooked in Cretan villas, French ski lodges, and London movie director's rooms. Typical menus include eggs Benedict for breakfast, fettuccine Alfredo for lunch, and crab-stuffed dolphin for dinner. If one of your girlfriends is vegetarian, kosher, or partial to nothing but green eggs and ham, just tell your yacht broker, who will match you with an accommodating chef.

Most yachts are hired through brokers whose job it is to inspect the vessels and play matchmaker between crews and sailing wannabes. The range of options is immense. You can hire everything from Gary Hart's undoing, the *Monkey Business*, to an English j-boat that competed for top honors in the 1935 America's Cup. Ringing in at a gulping $60,000 per week plus expenses, the j-boat has four staterooms, a fireplace, and 200 tapes and compact discs; it requires three mates just to get the sail out of the locker.

Standard toys on yachts are dinghies, fishing equipment, snorkeling gear, barbecue grills, sailboards, and video cameras. Many have a TV/VCR/DVD in each cabin, telephone service, and fax capabilities.

Not so standard, but definitely available, are helicopter pads, gold swan-shaped bathroom fixtures, different china for each day of the week, four-wheel-drive

Suzukis (which you can drive onto the island of the day), darkrooms for developing your underwater photos, and pianos with built-in heaters to keep the keys from warping.

Other options are your own scuba instructor (some yachts specialize in transforming beginners into regular Jacques Cousteaus), your own marine biologist, or your own Beach Boy—although you'll have to wait for the latter service, because the band's charter yacht was one of dozens destroyed by a recent hurricane.

The best part of charter yachting is the flexibility. There's no such thing as a deadline or an itinerary. You and the gals can get up each morning, size up the wind conditions, and decide which island you'd like to sail toward.

Your only real job is to pity the rest of the world. But if you'd like, the captain is always willing to turn over the boat's controls. While crews will stay out of your hair (as much as is possible on a 50-by-15-foot space) if you want them to, they are always happy to offer years of at-sea expertise. They know, for example, where the fish are most likely to bite, which dockside eateries offer the most authentic cuisine, and which jellyfish is best to avoid.

Because the boats are smaller (unless you're cruising with King Fahd, whose 482-foot yacht houses a mosque and a 100-seat movie theater), you can sail right into pristine cays and islets that passengers of cruise ships can only wave at as they sail on to congested wharfs.

So how, you're undoubtedly wondering, do you sign up for all this fun? It's really not much harder than renting a car.

While ideal conditions would allow you and your girlfriends to inspect the boats and meet the crews yourself, yachts are at sea at least thirty weeks a year so that's not likely to happen. Which is why you need a yacht broker. Yacht brokers and yacht crews meet once or twice a year at conventions, and yes, the vessels are there for the brokers' scrutiny.

Lifestyles of the Dead but Still Remembered

Okay, so you didn't see Cameron Diaz or Drew Barrymore. Never fear. There is a guaranteed method for tracking stars, a tour that can't possibly go wrong. This guide to the graves of the rich and famous comes with a money-back guarantee. If you don't see the stars (or, more accurately, their graves), we'll give you your money back. Course, we can't promise looks fitting a magazine cover. Some of them have been "down under" for more than a century.

1. **JUDY GARLAND.** Dorothy's fan club still leaves fresh flower at her nondescript vault at Ferncliff Cemetery in Hartsdale, New York, 281 Sector (914–693–4700).
2. **JOAN CRAWFORD.** While you're at Ferncliff, might as well give your regards to girlfriend Joan Crawford, who's buried nearby in an unassuming vault where the name Steele (her husband Alfred M. Steele) gets top billing. You can pick up a map at the main mausoleum.
3. **MARILYN MONROE.** The most popular in a graveyard of stars, Marilyn's beige wall crypt at the north end of Westwood Village Memorial Park continues to lure admirers. There's even a bench opposite where you and the gals can pay homage. Other girlfriends nearby are Eve Arden, Natalie Wood, Fanny Brice, and Peggy Lee. It's found at 1218 Glendon Avenue, Los Angeles (800–966–5113).
4. **ERMA BOMBECK.** Erma's grave marker is a 29,000-pound boulder that was lugged by a flatbed truck from her home in Arizona to Dayton, Ohio, where she grew up. She was buried in the Woodland Cemetery and Arboretum at 118 North Woodland Avenue, (937–222–1431).
5. **SUSAN B. ANTHONY.** We can thank this girlfriend for giving us the right to vote. Unfortunately, she kicked the bucket before the Nineteenth Amendment actually got passed, but make sure you tell her while tipping your hat at her gravestone at the Susan B. Anthony Home at 17 Madison Street, Rochester, New York (716–235–6124).

> **6. LILLIAN GISH.** A star of the silent melodrama, Gish, who launched her career at age nine, had sixty years of stage, radio, TV, and movie work. You can see her vault at St. Bartholomew's Episcopal Church in Manhattan at 109 East 50th Street and Park Avenue (212–751–1616).
>
> **7. JACKIE KENNEDY.** Buried alongside some of the world's most powerful men (what's new? In life, she landed a president and a self-made mogul/millionaire), Jackie's grave overlooks the Potomac River in Arlington National Cemetery. It's found west of Memorial Bridge (703–697–2131).

Since most of the brokers are fronting for the same 300 yachts in the Caribbean, for example, the trick is to find someone you feel comfortable with. A good broker will know if the bathroom in the master bedroom has perfectly matched marble. Or the captain is a dyed-in-the-jock Cincinnati Reds fan.

The first clue that you've found a good broker is that she (80 percent are women) will ask a trillion personal questions. She'll want to know if any of you wears contacts (to make sure there's electricity for sterilization procedures), if all of you eat red meat, if you're seasoned sailors or rookies who will probably scratch yours when she inquires about a "head," and if you prefer to fish for shrimp or marlin. By the time you fill out the several-page questionnaire, your yacht broker will probably know more about you than your own mother.

If you want cheap and you and your girlfriends are competent enough sailors to man a 30- to 50-foot vessel, you can hire what is called bareboat. All the equipment is there, but you won't get a skipper or a first mate. You'll also save a good 20 to 30 percent.

Many charter companies maintain their own fleet of standardized vessels. These boats tend to be pretty homogeneous for the same reasons that Avis stocks its fleets with Chevys with automatic transmissions.

Yacht brokers who represent dozens of individual captains are most apt to charter a one-of-a-kind boat. The boats are a floating combination of investment, livelihood, and home for the captains. So if you need an excuse, look at your charter yacht vacation as a benevolence offered to humankind.

For more information, contact The Charter Yacht Brokers Association at www.cybacharters.com or contact SailAway Yacht Charter Consultants, 15605 Southwest 92 Avenue, Miami, FL 33157-1972 (800–724–5292 or www.1800sailaway.com).

2. Play Star Search in Aspen. Not that you have to search that hard. Don Johnson, Jack Nicholson, Goldie Hawn, Sally Field, and Michael Douglas are just a few of the stellar somebodies who have second (or third or fourth) homes in Aspen. In fact, one girlfriend I met in Aspen told me she went out looking for a quiet dinner one night and found herself wedged between Bruce Willis and the Trumps (needless to say, this was a few years ago) instead.

Although it's pretty uncool in Aspen to gape, point, or ask for autographs, you're apt to catch a glimpse of somebody you recognize at Little Nell, Mezzaluna, Cache Cache, or the Caribou Club. Look for the antlers. And if that doesn't work, try Sardy Field. That's where they park their private jets.

3. Pretty Woman R Us. For the ultimate in luxury getaways, think Regent Beverly Wilshire Hotel, in (where else?) Beverly Hills, California. Not only is it where *Pretty Woman* was filmed, but it's also just a short walk from Rodeo Drive. Warren Beatty lived in the Veranda suite for years. Elvis Presley, Eddie Murphy, and Elton John are just a few of the folks who have stayed there. To book a stay, call the Regent Beverly Wilshire Hotel at 9500 Wilshire Boulevard (310–275–5200).

4. *Choose the British Virgins over the American Virgin Isles.* The U.S. Virgin Islands are where Bill and Ethel from Muskogee, Oklahoma, go on their vacation. The British Virgin Islands are where Mel Gibson, Tom Brokaw, Robert De Niro, and Mick Jagger go.

Although the BVI (the correct term for people in the know) has just as much land and just as many islands as the USVI, it also has one-tenth the population. In other words, you're not going to find twenty-story condos blocking your view of the ocean or mouthy blackjack dealers tending a casino. In fact, the only thing boisterous in the BVI are the fish that swim the coral reefs in schools of bright neon.

Virgin Gorda, one of fifty islands in the BVI, is the perfect outpost for a relaxing and luxurious girlfriend getaway. From its peak you can see the entire archipelago that stretches from Puerto Rico to Anegada that fronts the world's third largest reef.

You'll find posh accommodations (Mary Jo Ryan at the Bitter End Yacht Club will even cross-pollinate a couple of hibiscus to match the colors of your suitcase), private beaches (I sailed by Savannah Bay—a half-mile beach that is one of the Caribbean's prettiest—on a Sunday morning and found a grand total of two people), and so many water toys that you'll definitely need to make a schedule.

Sailing is the sport of choice for most Virgin Gorda vacationers. If you're a beginner, you can take Sailing 101 classes at the Bitter End. And when you're ready, you can sail to Prickly Pear (it's close, perfect for your maiden voyage), Salt Island (nearby is the wreck of the *Rhone*, a British mail ship that—besides being a popular dive site—was featured in the Nick Nolte movie *The Deep*), Fallen Jerusalem, or any other of the islands in the BVI chain.

None of them is too far away and (who knows?) you might even catch a glimpse of somebody famous. Nearby Necker Island, a private island owned by Richard Branson (head of Virgin Records and Virgin Air), has been rented out to the likes of Oprah Winfrey, Princess Di, and Steven Spielberg. Nightly rate? Seventeen thousand dollars.

Better to catch glimpses of, however, are the humpback whales that migrate through the Drake Channel every January and February, the stars (they're so clear, you can almost play dot-to-dot), and the sunsets. The latter are especially striking in August when winds from Africa carry sand from the Sahara Desert, painting the skies in swatches of vibrant pinks, oranges, and reds.

Near Spanish Town, where you can catch open-air taxis (they're really benches bolted to the bed of a pickup), you'll find what people in the BVI call the world's "eighth wonder." The maps refer to it as "The Baths." Sea-worn boulders as big as your house jut out of the sea, forming a mysterious labyrinth that you can either snorkel or hike through.

For more information on Virgin Gorda, call BVI Tourism at 800–835–8530. Bitter End Yacht Club can be reached at 800–872–2392.

5. *Follow the Stars.* Superman in his skimpy blue tights will probably never make the cover of *GQ* magazine. His split personality, not to mention his annoying tendency to disappear into phone booths, makes him a prime candidate for the psychiatrist's couch. But when it comes to being romantic, his taste is impeccable. In  *Superman II*, he flew all the way to St. Lucia's Ladera Resort to find the perfect flower for his beloved Lois Lane.

He knew something that Oprah Winfrey, Harrison Ford, Raquel Welch, and John Cleese figured out a long time ago. This cozy resort that's perched 1,000 feet above sea level has the prettiest view in the Caribbean.

All nineteen suites and villas have an open west wall, meaning you don't have to look out a smudged window to see the island's signature twin peaks, the jungle, or the Caribbean sea. The two-story, three-bedroom villas have their own gardens and private pools fed by a waterfall, and many of the suites have open-air showers, Jacuzzis, banana trees, and an occasional visiting salamander or bat.

With views like this, you and your girlfriends may never want to get out of your four-poster bed (each one is covered with mosquito netting), but just in case, the resort also has a pool, a library, a botanical garden, and the prizewinning Dasheene's restaurant. Call 800-448-8355 or the resort directly at 758-459-7323.

6. Give Peace a Chance.

Remember when John Lennon and Yoko Ono initiated a press conference for world peace from their hotel bedroom? For eight days they staged a Bed-In for peace from the Amsterdam Hilton's Suite 902. Every day, they gave interviews to 150 journalists willing to interview them, snap photos, and convey their protest of the Vietnam War. You and your girlfriends can rent their very suite (it's called the John Lennon and Yoko Ono suite and even has the words of a song by John Lennon painted on the ceiling) for a trip to Amsterdam. The Van Gogh museum, the Rijksmuseum, and the canals are all within a ten-minute walk. Hilton Hotel, Apollolaan 138, Amsterdam, 1077 BG, Netherlands (00-31-20-7106000 or www.amsterdam.hilton.com).

True-Life Tales

The Price (and the Trip) Were Right

THE GIRLFRIENDS:
1. Melinda, a marketing manager from Plano, Texas.
2. Amy, Melinda's best friend from high school, now a stay-at-home mom.

THE MISSION: To win a coveted spot on *The Price Is Right*.

THE DESTINATION: Los Angeles, California.

THE GETAWAY *(as told by Melinda)*:
"Amy and I had lost touch but were able to get caught up over e-mail a few years ago. We'd missed so much! We'd both married, and she had just had her second daughter. We decided it would be a real treat to travel to L.A. together and try to make it onto *The Price Is Right*. We didn't just want to make contestants row—we were going for the showcase showdown!

"We spent a four-day weekend waltzing down Rodeo Drive, checking out the decorations for that weekends' Oscar Awards, driving around looking for celebrities, eating anything and everything in sight, and prepping for our big game-show day. Believe me, we did our research! We each made T-shirts—mine with sparkly letters spelling I (HEART) TPIR and hers with precious pics of her girls. We read everything about the show online and all of the small print on the back of our show tickets.

"The night before, we got into our PJs at 8:00 P.M. and watched the Oscars until we fell asleep. Having tickets isn't a guarantee that you'll make it into the audience; it's all first come, first served. So at 5:00 A.M. we staked out our spot in line.

"We spent the next several hours getting to know our neighbors, mostly stay-at-home moms or college students. After proving our eligibility to win all of those amazing prizes (I had my heart set on a new car) and getting our trademark name tags, we went through a sort of audition process.

"The producers took the potential audience members in groups of four or five and asked us to introduce ourselves. This is where you have to put on the charm and act obnoxiously peppy (remember, we got there at 5:00 A.M.) because this is when they choose the lucky few who will be invited to 'come on down.'

"At 3:00 P.M. we were led into the studio for taping to begin. Everyone had the same reaction—"Wow, this is a lot smaller than it looks on TV." Two hours and thousands of dollars in prizes later, taping concluded and Amy and I started to come down from our adrenaline high, sadly realizing that we were not going to make our big game-show debut that day.

"We did manage to make it into a few audience shots, and Amy asked Bob Barker to say hello to her girls, but it was no new car or plinko money. But it was great girl bonding time."

—Thanks to Melinda Bentley for providing this True-Life Tale.

• • • • • • • • • • • • • • • •

Stalking the Stars

THE GIRLFRIENDS:
1. Yours truly.
2. Sarah, a friend from college who is now a stay-at-home mom.

THE MISSION: To collect celebrity autographs.

THE DESTINATION: Where else but Aspen, Colorado, during ski season?

THE GETAWAY: My childhood was spent in small Kansas towns. Sarah, who had the good fortune to be born in Nebraska, birthplace of Henry Fonda and Johnny Carson, moved to Kansas when she was four. Needless to say, neither of us rubbed elbows with many movie stars.

In fact, the only brush with fame I remember (and believe me, I'd have remembered) was in fifth grade when the revamped Ink Spots, a group of semiprofessional has-beens, came to Ellsworth, Kansas (pop. 2,500) to sing their one hit, "If I Didn't Care."

The other close call came in eighth grade when Dad, after inadvertently sitting next to her on a Disneyland roller coaster, landed an autograph from Joanne Castle, Lawrence Welk's rinky-dink piano player.

Being thirty-four and full-grown adults didn't diminish our excitement over a trip to Aspen and the possibility of seeing a real live movie star. Aspen, if the tabloids are to be believed, is better equipped with stellar somebodies than Hollywood itself. This, after all, is where Jack Nicholson's kids are learning to play tennis, where Donald and Marla romped behind Ivana's back, and where ski jackets sell for more than my car.

Besides, Tom and Nicole were splitting up. Why shouldn't he choose Aspen as the spot to find sympathy?

The prospects looked good when we landed in Pitkin County Airport. There, shoved over to the side of the runway like a dented Chevette, was Sally Field's Learjet with an unbecoming hole in the fuselage. Not that she was there filling out insurance forms or anything, but even a movie star's wrecked airplane would impress the folks back in Ellsworth.

Five Fantasy Getaways

1. **A NIGHT AT THE PLAZA HOTEL.** If you and your girlfriend are always jockeying for position in the hotel bathrooms, consider a night in the Plaza's Presidential Suite. Not only does it have seven bathrooms, but it also features 7,800 square feet, two levels, and its own private maid, butler, and chauffeur who'll take you anywhere you want to go in a Rolls-Royce.
2. **RENT YOUR OWN ISLAND.** You and the gals will have the whole island to yourselves when you rent Guana, an 850-acre nature preserve in the British Virgin Islands. It has unspoiled beaches and fifteen guest rooms in white stone cottages.
3. **BE A BOND GIRL.** That's Bond as in James Bond. The three-bedroom villa where Ian Fleming wrote fourteen of his James Bond stories is now for rent on the north coast of Jamaica. It comes with a cook, a maid, a butler, and its own private beach.
4. **TAKE A RIDE ON THE ORIENT EXPRESS.** Of all the romantic railways in the world, few can match the service or the scenery of the Orient Express. The original ran from Paris to Venice. Today's version will transport you and your girlfriends from the temples and palaces of Singapore and Malaysia to the national wonders of Kuala Lumpur and Penang.
5. **SPEND A NIGHT AT THE OSCARS.** Or at least in the neighborhood at the Beverly Hills Hotel, which has catered to such girlfriends as Elizabeth Taylor and Marilyn Monroe. The hotel will even take you on a limo ride to Rodeo Drive. Be sure to have dinner at Spago or Morton's.

Our jeep-driving taxi driver told us he'd recently transported Goldie Hawn, Jack Nicholson, and Charles Bronson—who, he was sorry to report, looked nothing like the macho man of the movies.

Even the Snowqueen, the Victorian bed-and-breakfast where we stayed, maintained an air of celebrity. It was owned and managed by none other than Norma Dolle, former Tony Twin. The

Tony Twins, in case you don't remember TV commercials of the 1960s, were identical twin sisters, one of whom sported a Tony perm. The TV audience was challenged to decide which sister had the best hair (that is, the Tony perm). Norma's twin sister, Marge Babcock, by the way, ran the bed-and-breakfast next door.

Savvy enough to know Goldie and Kurt would never hang out at the $68-a-night Snowqueen, Sarah and I asked Norma for instructions to town, a needless query in such a small town, and for restaurant recommendations, another waste of time since there's no such thing as a bad restaurant in Aspen. And with one hundred of them—that's one for every eighty residents—to choose from, that's quite an accomplishment.

We stumbled into Ute City Banque, a popular eatery named for Aspen's first designation—Ute City. Before miners struck a thick vein of silver here, Ute Indians inhabited the valley near Roaring Fork River. Silver miners with their heavy wagons, boisterous drinking habits, and seven newspapers drove the Utes farther and farther downvalley. Finally, in 1884, the town was renamed Aspen for the locally prolific tree.

The Ute City Banque, although nearly as old as Aspen, was trendy. We were the only females without fur coats. Sarah and I took a seat in the bar to wait for our names to be called. We had just ordered a beer when who should walk in but Timothy Hutton.

Or at least it looked like Timothy Hutton. We tried not to stare, but it evidently didn't work because he eventually sauntered over, invited us to join him and his friends for dinner, and introduced himself as "Milton, a fluorocarbon salesman from Houston."

His entourage was friendly and we enjoyed the company, not to mention the shared bites of elk Wellington, barbecued shrimp in corn bread, and lobster bisque.

A magician came by (everyone's looking for a way to support themselves in a town with an average home price of $1 million) and showed us a few tricks. He borrowed watches and rings and, after contorting, hiding, and finding them again in unknown pockets, returned them unharmed.

Next day's ski lesson on Buttermilk Mountain was not much better. Rather than movie stars, our ski class consisted of a sixteen-year-old from Cleveland, an art gallery owner from St. Louis, and a New York couple who mastermind political campaigns for liberal politicians. I have to admit the company was stimulating, the lessons useful, and the ski instructor cute—but he still wasn't Tom Cruise.

That night, we wandered over to the Wheeler Opera House, where Aspen's noncelebrity citizenry was hosting a Winterskol fireworks party. Winterskol, as near as we could figure, is an annual winter carnival created some forty years ago to pump up the traditionally slow month of January. As at most festivals, there were fireworks, a parade, and a bunch of ski instructors zooming down the mountain with torches. But the most interesting feature, in my opinion, were the hundred golden retrievers wearing matching plaid coats.

The hors d'oeuvres at the party were tasty and while I still hadn't located anyone I'd ever seen on television, I *did* inadvertently bump into a Chicago editor I'd worked with and only met by telephone.

Even the Hotel Jerome, while elegant and historically charming, lacked the one thing we most coveted—somebody famous.

We skied three days at Aspen, sampling each of Aspen Ski Company's three mountains. Rumor had it that most of the stars ski Ajax, the foreboding giant that shadows the town. But to spot anyone—including your own mother—under all those ski clothes is too daunting a task even for eager Kansas rookies.

Alas, as our trip to Aspen drew to an end, we had to concede that while it offers marvelous skiing, unrivaled shopping, and breathtaking scenery, it is not the place to spot a celebrity.

But then, on the plane from Denver to Kansas City, Deron Cherry, a retired Kansas City Chief, sat right in front of us. And while it's not Tom Cruise's phone number, his autograph sure looks nice next to Joanne Castle's.

● ● ● ● ● ● ● ● ● ● ● ● ● ● ● ●

Accidental Get-Together

THE GIRLFRIENDS:
1. Amy, owner of Weirick Communications.
2. Kathleen, Amy's childhood friend, an attorney and stay-at-home mom.
3. Lisa 1, also an attorney who stays at home with her kids. She and Kathleen were neighbors until she moved to Kentucky.
4. Lisa 2, head of the Columbus Dispatch Newspapers in Education program.

THE MISSION: To get away from the kids and partake of a girls-only weekend.

THE DESTINATION: Cherry Valley Lodge (740–788–1200 or www.cherryvalleylodge.com), a lovely country lodge in Newark, Ohio, that has hosted Hal Holbrook, Dixie Carter, Jimmy Buffett, and Jennifer Garner, star of *Alias*.

THE GETAWAY *(as told by Amy):*
"As the mother of two- and three-year-old boys, I was *so* excited (and nervous) to slip away for a far-too-rare escape from the craziness of two toddlers, plus running both a home and a busy home-based business. I took advantage of Cherry Valley's awesome girls-only weekend. It includes a wine tasting, a fun pajama party, psychic readings, massages, and lots more.

"During the Saturday-morning exercise options, I opted to sleep in (also a rare treat) while my companion, Lisa 2, went on a morning walk.

"While getting my breakfast at the lavish buffet, I noticed two very sweaty, very thin, pretty women, one black haired and dark, the other blond and fair skinned, coming out of the Tae Bo class and heading for the food. I thought to myself: *That's why they are skinny and I am not. I slept in. They got up and exercised.*

"As I seated myself at an umbrella table in the sunny courtyard on what was the most breathtaking spring morning I can ever recall, the blonde walked by, smiled, and gushed, 'Isn't this great!' I laughed and agreed, allowing that I never get to enjoy my coffee, let alone read the paper in peace, and what a treat this is. She agreed and laughed along with me. Then she looked at me seriously and said, 'You look *so* familiar!'

"So we did the old, 'where do you work, shop, live, play, go to church, et cetera' thing for ten minutes, not coming up with the link. Finally I said, for no reason at all, 'My maiden name was Walters.' "She screamed: '*Amy Walters!* It's Kathleen Rummell!' We hugged and laughed hysterically.

"Kathleen had been my very best friend from kindergarten through fifth grade, when we lived just three blocks from each other. But as my hormones set in, I (as she put it) 'dumped her' to hang out with 'the cool girls.' I explained to her that I had a mad, wild crush on Chip Motil and since he hung out with the 'fast girls' (which in fifth grade at Catholic school means they played spin the bottle and smoked) and I knew I had to join them if I was to get my man. Sad, but true. (And yes, I did get my man. Thankfully, I only smoked until I started high school.)

"Anyway, Kathleen was also with a friend named Lisa, so all four of us spent the whole weekend laughing and telling stories and getting reacquainted.

"Since then, we get together once a month or so for lunch or drinks. We have even hooked up with some other women from our grade school for fun get-togethers. What a wonderful surprise reunion that was! I had not seen her in thirty years."

—*Thanks to Amy Weirick for providing this True-Life Tale.*

I bet you thought you were coming to the end of this book. Think again, girlfriend. This book will not be finished until these last few pages are filled in. With *your* getaway. It's one thing to read about a girlfriend getaway. It's a whole different hot tub taking your own. Now's the time to come up with a list of girlfriends and to plot a mission and a destination. Don't even think about closing this book! There are a lot of chapters yet to be written. So, now my true and loyal girlfriend, I turn the reins over to you. The story has just begun.

The beginning.

Your True-Life Tale
Journal Your Own Adventure

THE GIRLFRIENDS:
_____
_____

THE MISSION:
_____
_____

THE DESTINATION:
_____
_____

THE GETAWAY
_____
_____
_____
_____
_____
_____
_____
_____

TALKING: ★★★★

GAWKING: ★★★★

ROCKING: ★★★★

DOCKING: ★★★★

Your True-Life Tale
Journal Your Own Adventure

THE GIRLFRIENDS:
_____
_____

THE MISSION:
_____
_____

THE DESTINATION:
_____
_____

THE GETAWAY
_____
_____
_____
_____
_____
_____
_____

TALKING: ★★★★

GAWKING: ★★★★

ROCKING: ★★★★

DOCKING: ★★★★

Index

A
Abbey, 109–10, 116–17
Abbey of St. Walburga, 116
About.com, 51
Alexis Hotel, 7
Allegria Spa, 50
All Womens' Fly Fishing Derby, 70
Amsterdam Hilton, 149
April Point Resort, 71
ArizonaSpaGirls.com, 53–55
Arlington National Cemetery, 145
Aspen Ski Company, 155

B
Babes in the Backcountry, 66, 76
Baden Baden, 58
Bad Girl's Guide to the Open Road, 79
Bareboat, 145
Benedictine, 112, 116, 117
Berry, Carmen Renee, 93
Beverly Hills Hotel, 153
Big New Free Happy Unusual Life, A, 35, 105
Biking, mountain, 70
Bitter End Yacht Club, 147–48
Blue Note, 101–2
Boosler, Elayne, 121
British Virgin Islands (BVI), 147–48, 153
Buddhism, 111, Tibetan, 111, Zen, 108, 114
BVI Tourism, 148

C
Camping, 12–13, 33
Canyon Ranch, 46, 100–101
Charter Yacht Brokers Association, 146
"Cher Girlfriend Getaway" contest, 135
Cherry Valley Lodge, 156
Christian hermitage, 111
Cinematherapy, 33
Coolfont Resort, 118
Course in Miracles, 107–8
Crested Butte, 64
Cruise ships, 45–46, 141
Cunard cruise ship line, 46

D
Day's Inn, 129
Destination Spa Group, 51
Dirt Camp, 70
Divine Secrets of the Ya-Ya Sisterhood, 23
Divine Travel, 113
Dubai International Airport, 126

E
Episcopalian, 115
Estes, Clarissa Pinkola, 21

F
Fashion Update, 125

Feng Shui, 50
Ferncliff Cemetery, 144
Fifth World Pilgrimages, 116
Fishbein, Amy, 61
Fishing, fly, 70
Four Seasons Hotel, The, 7

G

Georgia O'Keefe's Ghost Ranch, 112
Georgia O'Keeffe Museum, 15
Gilman, Susan Jane, 4, 124
Girlfriends: Invisible Bonds, Enduring Ties, 93
Golden Door, the, 46, 48–49, 53
Golf, 9, 21, 61–63, 65–66, 70
Golf by the Sea, 70
Google.com, 108
Gregorian chants, 117
Guggenheim, 100

H

Hawaiian Volcanoes National Park, 112
Hazen, Janet, 93
Hearst Castle, 15
Heartland Spa, 49
Holiday Inn, 15, 22
Horseback riding, 69
Hotel Jerome, 155
Hotel Vintage Park, 7

I

Indianhead Mountain, 64
Innkeepers of St. Augustine, The, 8
Inn on the Alameda, the, 15–16
Inn on the Creek, 98

International School of Fly Fishing, 70
Iroquois Memorial Hospital, 49

J

Jewish hermitage, 111
Johnson, Anna, 23

K

Kidd, Sue Monk, 41
Kiss My Tiara: How to Rule the World as a Smartmouth Goddess, 4, 124

L

La Costa Resort and Spa, 57–58
Ladera Resort, 148
Lama Foundation, 108
Las Olas Surf Safaris, 65, 68
Lil Bit North Ranch, 69
Lyons Victorian Mansion, 7

M

Madame Tussaud's Wax Museum, 100
Maha Kumb Mela, 113
Mantra, 109
Marsh Harbor Inn, 70
Meditation, 47, 109, 113, 115
Metropolitan Hotel, 10, 140
Milagro Retreats, 69
Monastery, 108–10, 114, 116
Monastery of Christ in the Desert, 112–13
Monkey Business, 142
Motel 6, 94
Mount Bachelor Ski Resort, 65
Mount Calvary Monastery, 114

N
National Breast Cancer Coalition, 67
New Age, 111

O
Ojai Valley Inn, 51
O'Keefe, Georgia, 15, 112, 139
Oktoberfest, 5, 116
Orient Express, the, 153

P
Packages, hotel, 7, 140, spa, 51–52, sports, 66, 140
Painter's Lodge, 70–71
Palm Island Resort, 102
Park Hyatt Beaver Creek Resort, 50
Pendle Hill, 113–14
Peninsula Hotel, the, 131
Peske, Nancy K., 33
P.F. Chang's, 101
Pilates, 45, 48, 76
Plaza Hotel, 153
Postrio, 101
Poustinia, 109
Prophet Muskwa Lodge, 62

Q
Quakers, 113–14
Queen Mary 2, 46
Queen of Angels Monastery of Benedictine Sisters, 116

R
Ramada Inn, 97
Red Tent gatherings, 108–9
Regent Beverly Wilshire Hotel, 146
Rijksmuseum, 149
Rio Caliente, 49
Ritz-Carlton, 131
Road trips, 9, 79–91
Row As One, 70
Rowing, 70

S
Sacred circles, 25–26, 29–30
Sacred Journeys for Women, 111
Saddlebrook Resort and Spa, 52
SailAway Yacht Charter Consultants, 146
Sailing, 69, 147
Salter, Stephanie, 15
Seabourn Cruises, 45
Seasons Restaurant, 7
Sedona Racquet Club, 45
Shalom Prayer Center, 116
Shopping, 10, 121–33
Side Trips Retreats for Women, 66
Sierra-at-Tahoe, 72–73
Sipapu Resort, 64
Skiing, 4–5, 62, 64–67, 72–73, 76–77
Snowboarding, 65, 72–75, 77
Snowqueen, 153–54
Sol Day Spa, 59
Sonoma Mission Inn and Spa, 56
Spa, 7–8, 41–59, 63, 100–101, club, 45, cruise ship, 45, day, 46, destination, 46, 51, medispas, 49, mineral spring, 49, resort hotel, 50
SpaFinders, 46
Spa Ojai, 51

Spa treatments, homemade, 53–55
Spirituality, 9, 105–19
Sports, 9, 61–77
Steamboat Springs Resort, 59
Sufi, 111
Sugarbush, 64
Sunday River Resort, 64
Sunlight Mountain Resort, 67
Surfing, 9, 65, 68–69
Surf Sister, 68–69
Susan B. Anthony Home, 144
St. Bartholomew's Episcopal Church, 145

T

Tae Bo, 156
Tai Chi, 8, 48
Taize, 109
10,000 Waves, 15
Thalassotherapy, 48, 52
Three Black Skirts, 23
Traeder, Tamara, 93
Trappist monks, 107
Truth About Girlfriends, The, 61
Tuttle, Cameron, 79

V

Van Gogh Museum, 149
Venetian Hotel, the, 99–102

W

Walnut Valley Bluegrass Festival, 32, 34
West, Beverly, 33
Westwood Village Memorial Park, 144
Wheeler Opera House, 155
Whistler's Pan Pacific Lodge, 128
Winter Park, 66–67
Winterskol, 155
Wise, Nina, 35, 105
Womanship, 69
Women Who Run with the Wolves, 21
Woodland Cemetery and Arboretum, 144
Wood Valley Temple and Retreat Center, 111

Y

Yacht brokers, 143, 145–46
Yacht, chartered, 141–43, 145–46
Yoga, 4, 7–8, 42, 45, 48, 57–58, 66, 68, 70, 77, 111, 113, 116, 131

Z

Zen Mountain Monastery, 108, 114

About the Author

Pam Grout is the author of ten books including *Living Big*, *Art and Soul*, and Globe Pequot's own *Kansas Curiosities*. Although she has occasionally traveled with men (including a trip to New Zealand where a former boyfriend refused to talk to her for an entire 48 hours), her most memorable getaways are those she has taken with her many assorted girlfriends. Her best girlfriend is her nine-year-old daughter, Tasman Grout, with whom she lives in Lawrence, Kansas.

More Food for Thought...

TRAVELING SOLO, 4th ed.
(0-7627-2664-4)

WILD WRITING WOMEN
Stories of World Travel
(0-7627-2377-7)

100 BEST SPAS OF THE WORLD, 2nd ed.
(0-7627-2473-0)

GILDED GIRLS
Women Entertainers of the Old West
(0-7627-2679-2)

YOGA WISDOM, Lyons
(1-58574-709-2)

BABES IN THE WOODS
*The Woman's Guide to Eating Well,
Sleeping Well, and Having Fun
in the Backcountry*
(0-7627-2530-3)

Available at your favorite booksellers
www.GlobePequot.com